# BOXSTER

**AUTHORS:**
CLAUSPETER BECKER
JÜRGEN LEWANDOWSKI
HERBERT VÖLKER

**PHOTOS:**
CHRISTOPH BAUER
DIETER BLUM
PETER VANN

**DELIUS KLASING**

Published by Dr. Ing. h.c. F. Porsche AG, Public Affairs and Press Department, Anton Hunger.

ISBN 3-7688-0966-8

© Copyright by Delius, Klasing & Co., Bielefeld

Additional work: Margit Askevold, Ines Deckstein, Klaus Parr, Klaus Steckkönig.

English translations: Colin Brazier, Munich
Layout: Sandra Kaiser, Hanstedt
Photographs: Christoph Bauer, Dieter Blum, Peter Vann, Porsche works photographs.
Editorial assistance: Monika Lewandowski
Repro: Zerreiss GmbH, Grafische Betriebe, Nuremberg
Printing: Kunst- und Werbedruck K+W, Bad Oeynhausen

Printed in Germany, 1996

All rights reserved. Not to be reproduced, transmitted as data or copied either manually or with the aid of electronic or mechanical systems (including photo-copying, recording on tape and data storage) without the publisher's express permission.

# Contents

| | |
|---|---|
| Classic Porsche Tradition in a Modern Interpretation | 7 |
| Seeing Things in the Right Light | 35 |
| The Boxster's Technical Background | 57 |
| Accomplishing the Impossible | 73 |
| Porsche on Ice | 83 |
| Advertising – an Essential Ingredient | 95 |
| A Man and a Vision | 113 |
| Meeting Points | 129 |
| The Practical Application of Beauty | 155 |
| Technical Data | 159 |
| Pictures | 160 |

# Classic Porsche Tradition in a Modern Interpretation

When after many years, Porsche creates a totally new car, every drawing and every aspect of the design inherits something quite priceless: the cumulative experience that means leadership for this manufacturer of sports cars.

We're sports car specialists. We've been building them for about fifty years, and we have a lead in know-how that nobody can take away from us." Wendelin Wiedeking, Porsche's chief executive, has no doubt that the new Boxster represents the finest Porsche tradition, and will further enhance his company's reputation.

Close observers of the fortunes of the Zuffenhausen-based company in recent and not-so-recent years will have seen the ups and downs of the world economy precisely reflected in Porsche's annual reports and balance sheets: the first German "economic miracle", the rise and fall of the US dollar, the oil crisis and the end of the belief in unrestricted mobility for evermore. There were also periods when a seemingly insatiable US market generated record sales volumes, and the yuppies of the late nineteen-eighties seemed to have endless supplies of cash. Then came the early nineties, money became short again and the "lean years" were suddenly upon us. Porsche's order book reflected this development just as it had all the others previously.

Sometimes it is a curse, sometimes a blessing for a small, exclusive manufacturer to live off the proceeds of a limited sales volume. Scarcity value makes the product attractive, but high prices confine its appeal in practice to a relatively small group of potential customers, who can change their investment priorities almost overnight if the climate begins to blow cold.

"There were times in the company's history when it was much too seriously affected by these market cycles," says Wiedeking. From the very moment the Boxster project was first mooted, he was well aware "that we had to develop a new model that would move our company, with its exclusive market-niche products, away from the peaks and troughs of economic fluctuation."

A product, in other words, that would appeal to a wider and younger target group, and establish a broader sales foundation for this small company with its great name – one that would enable it to maintain its independence. The product would have to be a car that would involve this new, younger public actively with the brand and also one that would win the hearts of more women drivers.

Four years ago, therefore, the company's executives came together with the intention of drafting an initial outline of what would have to be both an alternative and a complement to the all-powerful 911 model. For Horst Marchart, Porsche's technical director, "the Boxster was the chance we had ignored for many years to create a new and entirely individual product. A car that could only be a Porsche from the first moment on."

This statement becomes easier to understand if we look back at the circumstances in which earlier developments took place – all too often as joint projects with Volkswagen, and therefore suffering from a certain lack of internal acceptance despite the commercial success which these cars frequently enjoyed.

As the Porsche Development Center in Weissach began to map out the overall specification for the new Porsche

**For a small, exclusive manufacturer, having to live from a limited sales volume can be both a blessing and a curse**

model, it was already evident that the 968 and 928 models were reaching the end of their useful life. The termination of these two model lines, however, was at the same time a clue to what form the new car should take. It had to be a pure two-seater once again, the engine had to move back from the front to where it rightfully belonged, ahead of the rear axle – and the car's appearance had to clearly confirm its sporting character. "First of all, we are the sports car specialists," says Wiedeking, "and secondly the young people we're aiming for want a car to have this kind of good looks." In other words, the Boxster would have to set itself apart quite clearly from the 911 models: it would have to look different but so that there could be absolutely no doubt as to it being a "genuine Porsche".

Porsche is of course in the fortunate position of being able to look back on a most varied and successful history, and can therefore select more or less at will from the many landmarks it has set up in automobile design and engineering. This made it somewhat easier to walk the tightrope between the eternally young 911, the "living legend", and the desire to keep the past alive in a totally different visual form.

"Our first thoughts were naturally enough directed towards our own past history," Horst Marchart says. "We knew that we would have to quote from the past in the new Boxster, not just because nostalgia happens to be fashionable but because this is the only way for a company like Porsche to remain true to its principles – to know its own history and how it should be interpreted."

The first sketches began to accumulate in Weissach, but there was also another point that the project team had to take into account: the need to make as many of the new car's parts as possible identical with those used in the 911. Porsche needed no reminder that its model diversity in recent years had often involved complex and much too expensive production routines. Placing the engine ahead of the rear axle was clearly a requirement that was in line with this parts-sharing policy. Another advantage that had the effect of making the decision easier: the ability to boost production of one model or the other and so become more capable of responding to changes in market demand.

"By taking a great many identical components and using them to build two totally different cars we can keep production running close to the ideal output figure!" For Wendelin Wiedeking, who inherited a product program consisting of three quite different model lines with four-, six- and eight-cylinder engines, this prospect must be rather like a dream come true.

As far as the mid-engine concept is concerned, the echoes from almost fifty years of Porsche automobile construction are there to see. The very first genuine Porsche, which took to the road on June 8, 1948 in Austria, had its engine right there – in front of the rear axle. Later, on October 1, 1953 at the Paris Motor Show, Porsche unveiled the 550, the pioneer of an original and highly successful racing-car category. It was not only mid-engined but also possessed styling of such captivating beauty as to have lost nothing of its youthfulness, purity and elegance in the intervening years.

The people who build sports cars in Zuffenhausen have never given way to passing fashion. For them, the overused but basically true dictum that "form follows function" was always totally self-evident – almost as if it had been first coined on the Porsche assembly lines. "'Honesty' has always been one of the terms that we feel could be applied to our products – and functionality too," says Horst Marchart. The designers and technical people working on the new model under his leadership knew that their task was to create a modern classic, a car that would be free from any reliance on short-lived fashion and one that would act as a logical partner to the 911.

When it came to finalizing the new car's shape, the team headed by chief designer Harm Lagaay had a very clear picture of how the Boxster's target group would be made up: with an average age of 35, its members are about ten years younger than potential 911 buyers, and in addition the proportion of women owners is expected to double from the current figure of 15 percent to about 30 percent. In awareness of this, the new model clearly had to satisfy certain specific requirements: slightly more "fashionable", fewer classical outlines, for instance. The explanation for this: the typical 911 driver tends to be something of an introvert, but the potential Boxster owner will be someone not averse to making a bolder public statement. Furthermore, the Boxster age-group is still much more actively interested in leisure sport: travel, mountain-biking, surfing and snow-boarding are among the typical hobbies quoted.

It was naturally also known, for example, that women drivers, though interested in classical and innovative design, pay particular attention to practicality and to the car's suitability for everyday use. This has been reflected from the start in such features as a soft top that fits perfectly and is effortless to operate, doors that open to a wide angle, plenty of internal storage space and the two unusually large trunk compartments at front and rear.

With the target-group definition and the technical requirement specification as starting points, the car's appearance quickly began to take shape. Since all major automobile manufacturers like to sample public opinion these days, Porsche decided at relatively short notice in the fall of 1992 to exhibit the new model as a design study at the Detroit Motor Show, which was held in January 1993. Visitors and the media alike were delighted and impressed, despite having seen only a far from definitive version. This triumphant preview was the confirmation that Porsche's management were hoping for: that the new model would establish itself as an independent concept alongside the 911.

**The mid-engined concept that was finally chosen had some great forebears – Porsche's first-ever car in 1948 had its engine ahead of the rear axle**

In the weeks and months following the first public showing of this design study, Porsche dealers were inundated with no fewer than 10,000 orders. Potential customers had clearly identified the difference between Boxster and 911, and it was equally obvious that the target price would reflect this difference too. "76,500 Marks are certainly not too much for a Porsche," says Wendelin Wiedeking, adding that "the people who buy sports cars always prefer to own the "genuine article." They can get power elsewhere too – but they also want emotion, history and heritage. This is a blend that only Porsche can offer."

Detroit was also where Porsche revealed the name chosen for the new car: Boxster, an amusing, easily remembered combination of the two classic terms Boxer and Speedster. A name that caught on very rapidly, and helped for the next three years to publicize a car that scarcely anyone had yet seen! "We had no intention of exhibiting developed versions of our design study simply to keep people talking about the Boxster," declares Horst Marchart, who was convinced from the start that "the Boxster's first appearance in Detroit was sufficient proof that we would shortly be launching an interesting, attractive new model. We are content with the curiosity people have shown about our new product." The determined efforts made by prototype-hunters to capture the definitive shape on film in any way possible are evidence enough of the fascination it exerts.

As long ago as that successful first appearance in Detroit, it was obvious that the Boxster concept was right for Porsche's future. The overwhelmingly favorable response supplied just the additional motivation that the development team needed to spur it on. From that moment, everyone was more convinced than ever that the concept was correct – which made the many hours of overtime they were obliged to work much easier to endure.

For a relatively small company such as Porsche, it was far from easy to create a completely new product capable of standing up to comparison with the legendary 911, and fully entitled to bear the Porsche name alongside it. Wendelin Wiedeking, his fellow-directors and their development team have worked unceasingly to perfect their new Boxster concept. The result is most certainly the "genuine Porsche" they were aiming for, combining dynamic handling with distinguished good looks, suitability for day-to-day driving and practical value in the same supremely confident way that this manufacturer's products have always done. Remember the Chairman's words which we quoted at the beginning? "We're sports car specialists. We've been building them for about fifty years, and we have a lead in know-how that nobody can take away from us."

And if anyone should ask what that lead looks like in reality, a glance at the Boxster provides the answer.

JÜRGEN LEWANDOWSKI

A character-study from the concept phase: the typical curves and proportions are already evident, and also the designer's clear preference for a central exhaust tailpipe.

A transparent plastic model, complete with hardtop and 17-inch wheels – this represents the Boxster in its final form. Next to it, a clay model on which parts were shaped for the Tequipment program.

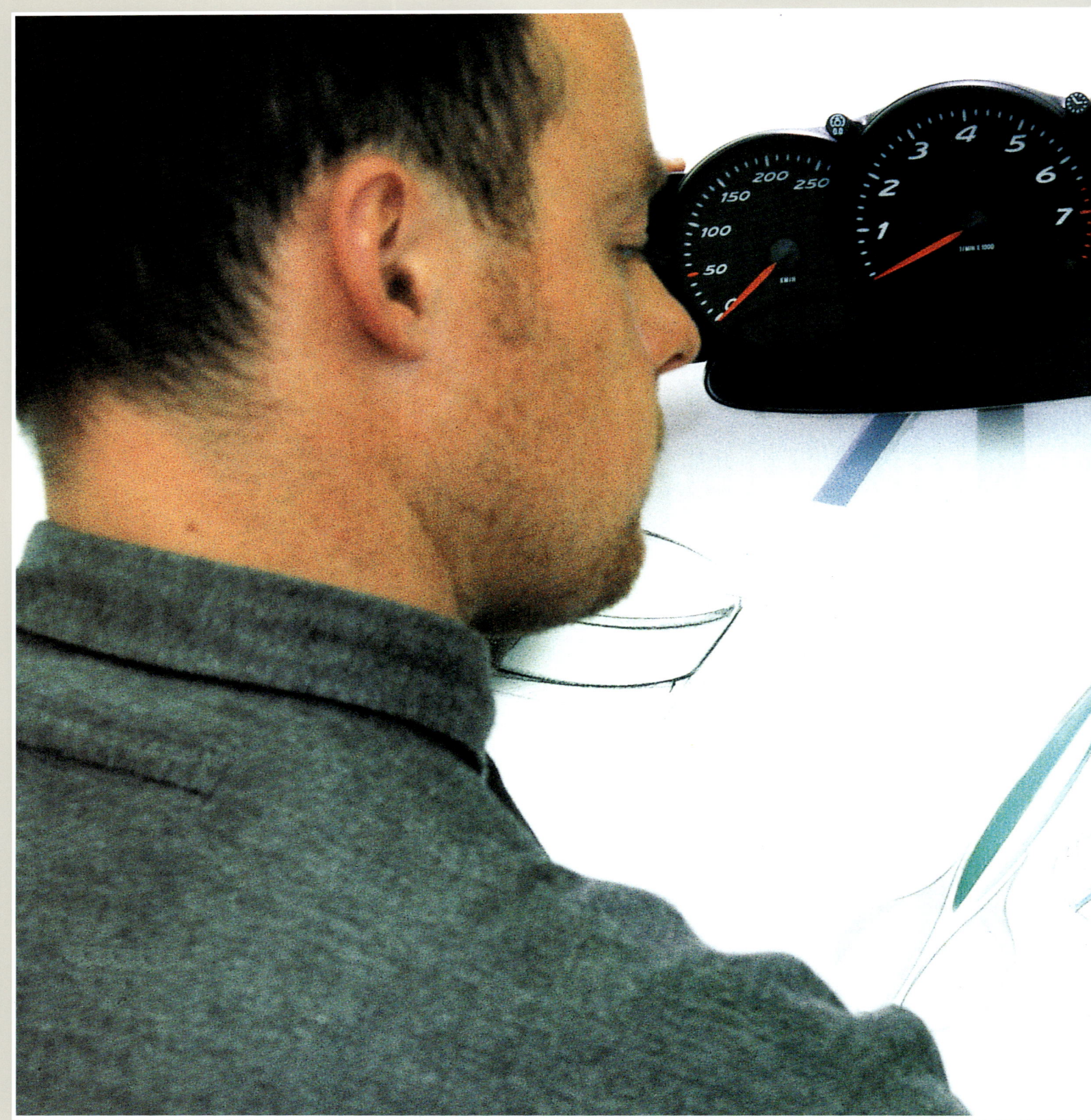

The very smallest details treated with affection: new Porsche instrument needles after a mere 22 years. Within the delicate "island" forms and the flowing shape they create, the dials have not so much a graphic effect as that of a three-dimensional body.

The Boxster's rear end from an unusual perspective, with the spoiler extended. It interrupts the airflow and reduces drag at high speeds.

# Seeing Things in the Right Light

Its character is expressed in its stance and muscle play, in the flowing curves, in the rhythm of stretching and acceleration, and suddenly everything is new: how the designer's pen found its subject. The design story of the Boxster.

*The way you look at a car has a lot to do with enthusiasm, even with passion and love. It's a little bit like real life.*

"Sweetheart?"
"Hm?"
"Are you listening?"
"Mm."
"What is it that you love the most about me? Tell me."
"You already know."
"And what comes after that?"
"Hm. Your intelligence. – Oo!"
"No, really."
"Your left earlobe."
"Why? Tell me why."
"In a little while."
"Why?"
"I have to think about it."

*So much for the introduction: A short story about design and its reception.*

Designers have mid-engined dreams about freedom, customers who are willing to make sacrifices, and exciting dramaturgy that likes to play with distributions of mass: accent on the nose, on the rear.

There was nothing like that in the 1992 spring selection for the design department, which is called "Style Porsche". The requirements they had to meet sounded like this:
- The everyday suitability of a fully-fledged Porsche, let's say the 911.
- The kind of seat dimensions and space that the new giants need ("People are getting bigger and we want some peace and quiet for the next 15 years," is the story. "But why does everybody have to play golf?")
- The long wheelbase the engineers have decided on.
- The tense harmony of the aerodynamic engineers.

And so the "mid-engine fantasy" became the "mid-engine reality".

If anyone thought they could make yet another Porsche without a steeply angled tail, they had another problem on their hands – a far from small one.

The family resemblance would have to show through – but how much?

Everyone expects the next Porsche to look exactly like the current one, but completely different. And if people can't see that the new one is really the old one, they get nervous and start to sulk.

Porsche's design philosophy has a lot to do with form, with that one specific form that needs no explanation. It may have been derived from the function of a rear-engined coupé, but it has gained the power and the magic of an icon. It has developed well beyond the rear engine and made itself independent. It has to be borne in mind for every kind of Porsche with four wheels. The immediate recognition of the old form is part of the plan. Anyone who violates this rule is punished by history.

Design philosophy, however, is not just about a car's construction. The character inherited from the parental home is expressed in its stance and muscle play, in the curves that move back and forth, in the rhythm of stretching and acceleration. It is revealed in the lines and joints, and how the surfaces come together. The character of the car is also about how the highlights pick out the peaks. And it is about the places where the tokens of love are found, the symbols of intimate familiarity.

Designers call this whole package of subtleties the "formal language". Here at Porsche it has been cultivated for the last forty years – always in a high-tech environment that allows no mannerisms.

That is why "Porsche" is one of the clearest languages that a car can speak to us in.

**Porsche's design philosophy derives from the function of a rear-engined coupé, but has acquired the power and magic of an icon**

What the strategists call target specifications reach the designers from the engineers in the form of a "package". The package is a skeleton including technical components, ergonomic measurements and the information that determines how they all relate to one another. The designers are allowed to get angry about all this, and sometimes they even get their way ("Dear colleague, with this wheelbase the best I can build you is a rubber boat").

It does not take long to create an initial package that suffices to get the design moving, but evolution takes considerably more time. The people at "Style Porsche" knew what was going on as early as March 1992. Chief designer Harm Lagaay appointed six of his team (each with four modelers) to work on the Boxster in a kind of elimination contest. Amazingly, this process works just as we outsiders think it should: a lot of computer work (CAD, of course), hundreds and hundreds of sketches, boards with wondrous outlines in tape, quarter-scale clay models, a lot of wonder tape again, full-scale models (designer A does the left side, designer B the right), and at the end, everyone makes a complete one.

In a separate room, a seventh designer was working on the Boxster: Grant Larson. He had a simplified package with fewer prescribed details. It still had to be a mid-engine, but the future owner did not have to be a giant and did not want to play golf. The nose could be shorter, the hood lower, the air inlet could be wherever it looked best. The idea was to present the vision of the Boxster, to inspire the other guys despite the burden of their target specifications, to seduce them constantly in the direction of beauty. As early as the summer of 1992, Grant Larson's free exercise had become so attractive that seduction towards beauty became an issue of its own. The decision was made to finish the design study for the 1993 Detroit Motor Show.

**An idyllic scene in the studio yard: the 1993 show car in front of the production version, here still seen as a clay model with plastic foil covering.**

Simultaneously with the show car, work continued on the full packages, and through constant comparisons it became clear that – disregarding the varying degrees of design freedom for a moment – the study had something that all the others did not. The fantasy car, transformed temporarily into an exhibition piece, gained more and more internal momentum.

That "something special", which can be the deciding factor at such cross-roads in the development process, adds an additional element to the idea, to the form and to the formal language as well: like a painter's brushstroke, a pianist's touch, a poet's melody or a composer's phrase, it defies definition. We tend to speak of the "line" – and whether it has expressed its subject or not.

Grant Larson's line was an internal hit, and even before the show car went on display in Detroit, it changed from a side issue to central issue at Porsche's Weissach development center and was confronted with the actual package.

The engineers and production people too were subjected more and more to the seduction of beauty, to the charisma of this bird of paradise. This made some changes in the package possible, and by the spring of 1993 form and function had grown together.

Right in the middle of this process, Detroit happened. It was a triumph, a victory right from the start. The world loved the idea of the Porsche Boxster.

In the exuberance of the first rendezvous, some tended to forget the emphasis on the "Concept Car".

In Weissach the design work was now tied up neatly. The comparison stage was brought to an end. Grant Larson and two design engineers now stepped into the mainstream of the action.

The actual Boxster could not be a mere 410 centimeters long, no matter how cute it would then look. Safety, space and cooling were the arguments against it, and they determined the front-end measurements.

A development plan with plans for a fully-grown rear trunk only had space for a fuel tank up front, and thus crash energy absorption became a crucial safety issue with no room for negotiation or compromises.

The evolution of Porsche headlights, fenders and joint-line patterns over the years (356, three 911 models, Boxster). The relationship between the individual body elements has not changed, but in combination they have become steadily more direct, compact and modern.

The final product is a 431 cm long car with no compromises in function, safety or space. The design signals mid-engine, 911 evolution, a new accent for the soft top and hardtop, and a wonderful alternative to the wedge-shape back that we have seen enough of. It expresses itself in the Porsche language and runs with the wind ... with the record drag coefficient for convertibles of 0.31.

Emergence of the Boxster's front end from the heritage of the 911 was logical and fitting: the classic Porsche landscape with its high side flanks is unmistakable – that very specific relationship between the fenders, the position of the headlights and the height of the trunk lid.

The radiators, which were moved far forward, represented the greatest design problem; they determined the distance from the front wheel arch to the headlights. A steeper slope than Porsche normally uses made it possible for the overhang to appear shorter and lighter.

The shark mouth of the concept car was not possible due to the two radiators the car now had, and would also not have been practicable on account of the ramp angle. Neither would the central air inlet have been suitable, and therefore the two elongated air inlets set the theme for the dual radiators. Below the number plate there is space for an additional opening to allow heat from the Tiptronic transmission to escape.

A totally new element within familiar territory is the neat S described by the trunk lid joint; the designers call this "stroke and counter-stroke". It was created on the show car, charmed Detroit, did not cause much enthusiasm among the production people, but was accepted anyway. It is a subtle detail, visible only to the trained eye. Usually on a Porsche the joint between the rear fender and the trunk lid runs along the valley, precisely at the lowest point, tapering towards the firewall, but in a straight line. The new S-stroke brings the terrain alive; the path not only runs along the mountain peaks but also criss-crosses them in an extremely charming fashion.

We shouldn't talk it to death, nor emphasize it too much even in a picture; it is a very three-dimensional affair, and pleasant to the touch.

Evolution of the headlight design from the 911 heritage is more visually striking and a very important detail for the character of the Boxster front end. Existing graphic forms find each other in a new arrangement and effortlessly integrate the associated functions: an island for headlights, direction indicators and fog lights in a theme based on the ellipse.

Designers don't like it if you are absorbed in contemplating their newest creation and then risk mentioning an ancient name.

"Is it OK if the Jaguar XK 120 comes to mind?"

"It can certainly come to mind," says Harm Lagaay, "it had a pronounced dome. And the Boxster also has a beautiful soft top and hardtop. Some beautiful things come to a stop at some point, but then they can be picked up and developed further. We interpreted this classic dome-type roadster element in a totally new soft top version and then expressed both in Porsche's formal language."

This is a soft-top mechanism that has never before been seen on a convertible, a dynamic Z – elegant, because it does not rear up to an overpowering height. Instead of simply folding back, the Boxster soft top folds up in itself three times during the backward motion, so that its outer surface is still visible in the stored position – which opens up new areas of fantasy for the design:

The soft top is still visible when it is put away, recalling the classic tonneau-cover look and influencing the visual proportions which – particularly for a mid-engine two-seater – are quite different from what one might expect. The

**Scarcely definable, like the painter's brushstroke or the pianist's touch: the element that accompanies idea and form**

visual size of the interior can be influenced by the change between the body color (the cover of the soft-top compartment) and the color of the soft top itself. If the latter had been completely concealed, it would have created different proportions. This can be seen on the Detroit car (the show car was designed for a conventional soft-top mechanism which would probably have made fastback-type dimensions necessary).

Right from the start the independent appearance of the hardtop Boxster played an important role. It is not a geometric form, but rather the tension lines of the round roof become visible like tendons. The transition from the rear window to the main body gains power from movement. The line swings with the form and makes it more lively.

One of the next steps in the typical Porsche formal language is expressed in the graphics of the door gap lines – at its clearest in the form of the arch that runs out of the B-pillar and over the shoulder. The graphics of the front joint line may take you all the way back to the 356.

The wedge shape and swelling rear end were much more popular than they are today during the design phase that was decisive for the Boxster's styling, and we are not just talking about the aerodynamic engineers and their unchanging love for a high spoiler line.

Harm Lagaay and the majority of the people from "Style Porsche" had the feeling that the time was ripe to experience a car without a rising rear end – even with Porsche tradition left out of consideration.

One thing was clear from the start: even the name "Porsche Boxster" triggered associations with the Spyder from the 1950s: the small one, the light one, the cozy and feisty one, and everything you ever wanted to know about James Dean.

No one, however, had a retro-design à la Spyder or RSK in mind. Retro-design in the sense of "art for art's sake" was never valued very highly at Porsche in view of the way the company sees itself and its relationship with technology.

**The visions of how the Boxster tail could have looked: "classic", "steep and aerodynamic" and finally a combination of typical Porsche forms and proportions.**

Harm Lagaay: "Cars from those days have become transfigured. They are not reproducible: neither their small size, nor their level of discomfort, nor any other aspect of their construction. We would just be destroying a legend if we put a Spyder from the 1950s next to a modern product."

The non-rising tail asserted itself at Porsche as a modern solution, as a pleasant contrast to the fashion (maybe now getting a little out of date?) for bulbous rear ends. Should you think of the Porsche Spyder and the legendary RSK, and probably do so with pleasure, this is an elegant intricacy of only marginal utility. The trunk lid is again lower than the fenders – typical Porsche tradition, reinterpreted with extended forms and new visual effects.

In line with the design-is-function principle, side air inlets are an important feature of mid-engined cars, even if they do not directly serve the radiators. In the case of the Boxster, the inlets were kept appropriately small (only for ventilation of the engine compartment), but the visual accent is still striking. The spectacular low-flying openings on the concept car would be exposed to too much damage from flying stones to be usable in everyday life.

The engineers wanted twin exhaust tailpipes, but the designers wouldn't give up on their idea of a central pipe, and hid the two siamezed pipes in an oval end unit.

A new ergonomic concept for the "generation of giants" in the sports car cockpit, and therefore a new basic layout for the arrangements: keep what is good, question much.

Should intimacy be strengthened or distance created? As far as distance - which is particularly sensitive for sports cars - is concerned, there is hardly a better example than the 911; the sense of space in the Boxster is related to it in spirit.

Full integration (a flowing transition from one element to the next) or not, is the next question. The Boxster relies on the lightness of islands that combine in a free-flowing form. Fluent, light and with just a hint of poetry is how the designer describes it.

"Poetic, really?"

"Well that's a little bit too strong, but it still expresses what I wanted to distance myself from."

The "main island" is the instrument panel, that seems almost to float freely in the air.

The choice of color enables the Boxster archipelago to express itself more strongly or less so (dark color).

The strong central statement made by the instruments defines its character. The departure from the upper section / border/ lower section arrangement sets the entire interior in motion: "if we had not made the dashboard as we did, then the doors would not look like they do either, and neither would the center console." (Kulla).

The dials were not pulled together just for visual effect, but rather to create a three-dimensional body. The "roof", the "bridge" are shaded in with a light hand, comparable to a motorcycle.

In almost all cars that have the engine up front, a center console causes the dashboard and center tunnel to grow together – often for reasons of both design and of function. The mid-engine car can do without this effect and leave the space more open. The Boxster makes use of this opportunity. Additional elements (designers call them "satellites") can, if desired, be used to make a vertical unit with all its practical advantages (shelf, audio, monitor screen, telephone). In the rear section there is already a lockable storage compartment anyway. The flow is divided up by graphic effects. The form is continuous, but color contrast emphasizes the different materials.

How about the instrument needles? Surely a dial is a dial is a dial ...? But it lives and wants to be seen. "You wouldn't believe," the designer said, "what a battle it is to design a new instrument needle and then get it accepted. It's like football or driving a car: everybody knows something about it. Everybody is some kind of instrument dial specialist and has their own opinion: make the needle a little bit more pointy, or a little bit blunter. But for every jacket there are only certain buttons that match." Anyway, we now have new Porsche instrument-dial needles. Very exciting after 22 years.

No need to explain that the tachometer is no longer needed to save us from over-revving the engine. Nevertheless, in the Boxster it is the king of the instruments: the nostalgia of gear shifts at the perfect moment, though everyone can interpret it however they choose.

The kids can't believe it (Look, 250!). Nowadays, increments of fifty on the speedometer are allowed only on a secondary system. The required increments of twenty appear on the permanent digital display.

Designers, engineers, modelers: the Porsche Boxster styling team.

About the typography: a type of lettering called Carrera. It is from the fifties, went out of date in the seventies, and is now getting ready for the next millennium – with a little help from Style Porsche: not every character has exactly the same slant. It's kind of like your own handwriting, OK?

A few words about the long farewell of the 911 switches. The concept, form, visual effect, and arrangement are all new. Every circle becomes an ellipse if seen from an angle. Motion is created through variation, even though the form stays neutral.

The form grows out of the surrounding surface without a transition, the contrast is accomplished through a change from shiny to matt. Wherever a small part has a particular form, it is gently highlighted with a shiny black finish – from the cap on the gear lever through the door opener and all the way to the light switch.

HERBERT VÖLKER

Driving tests don't only depend on artificially produced weather in the low-temperature test chamber: Porsches are tested in many different climatic zones, from well below zero beyond the Arctic Circle in Canada to the torrid heat of the Arizona desert in the USA.

Development work is actually a process of communication. The engineers discuss their results and measurements critically, usually in the presence of their silent colleague, the computer.

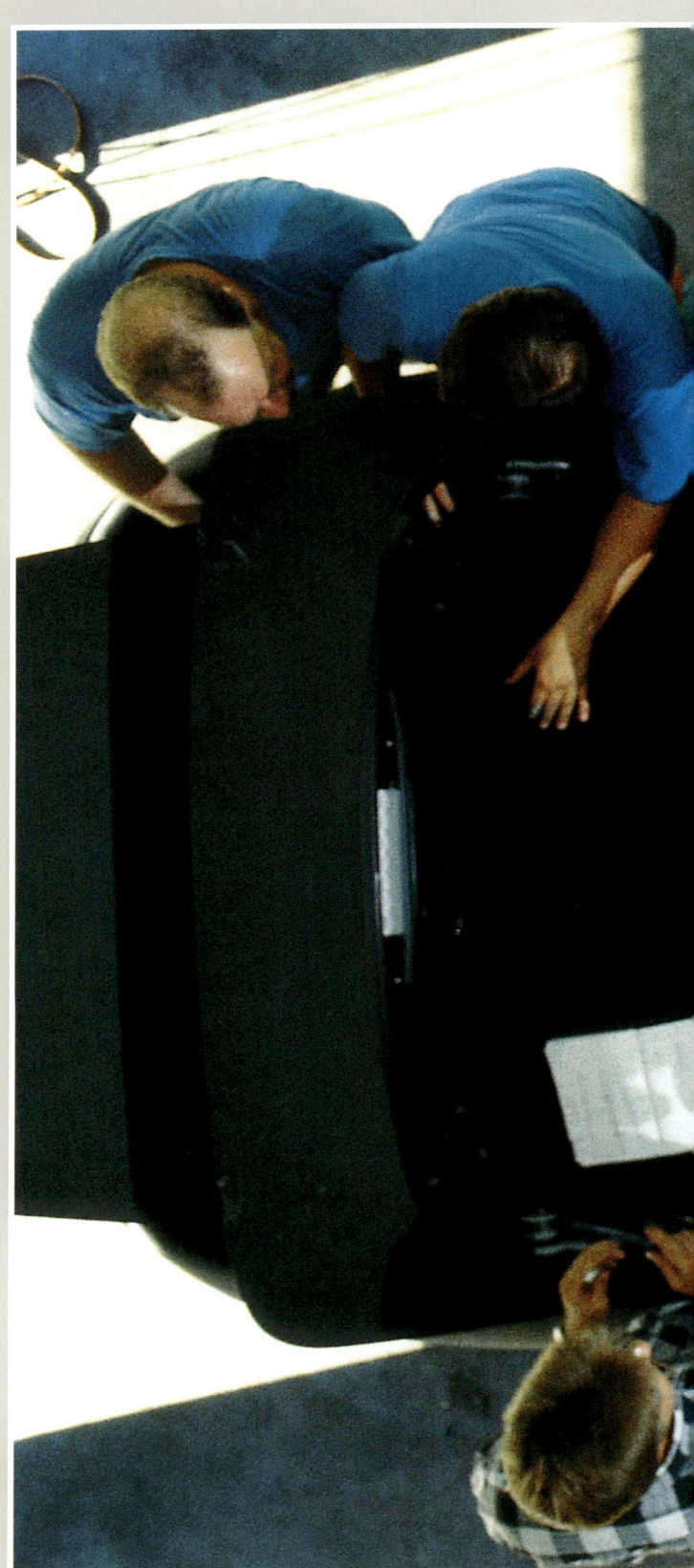

The wind tunnel is not just about aerodynamics. It is also needed to check operation of the cooling, heating and ventilation systems. Road-test results are confirmed by tough treatment on the road simulator.

Long before life-size prototypes exist, scale models are being tested in the small wind tunnel in order to obtain an initial impression of the quality of the designer's work.

# The Boxster's Technical Background

The flat-six, the celebrated opposed-cylinder engine that Porsche has used for more than 30 years, is hard to beat – unless you produce an even better flat-six like the one just premiered in the Boxster …!

In 1968, the year in which the students took to the streets and protested against an aging establishment with slogans such as "Trust nobody over thirty", the air-cooled horizontally opposed six-cylinder Porsche engine had scarcely reached elementary-school age and was immune to any such criticism. Now it has reached the age of thirty and is itself the object of a similar conflict of generations. Its friends trust it implicitly, and it is certainly far from suffering any form of senile decay, *but for Porsche's far-sighted engineers, the limits of its development are in sight*. However, a place of honor among classic automobile engine designs would seem to be certain.

In the words of Ulrich Schempp, who led development work on the Porsche 986: "In spite of all our respect for the existing engine, we could see the need for a new one that would uphold Porsche's authority in the engine design area for another lengthy period." But more than thirty years after the epoch-making 911 engine first saw the light of day, the disciplines associated with engine design have become far tougher. Peak power and torque are now merely two objectives among many others. Fuel consumption, exhaust emissions and compliance with noise-level regulations are now just as crucial. And the third challenge that Porsche's engine designers had to face was one of cost: the need to produce a top technological product at minimum expense.

"Our task was to design a far better engine but to make it at only a fraction of the cost of the previous one!" says Jürgen Kapfer, head of Boxster engine development. A fundamental conflict, typical of a modern engine specification. Of course, Porsche is in the Swabian region of Germany, famous for what we had better call its cautious attitude to money, but the horizontally-opposed layout was retained nonetheless, despite the extra cost involved in building a six-cylinder engine of this type – because it simply happens to be the best there is.

The radical departure from the air-cooled principle in favor of water cooling was inevitable in view of general technical developments in car engine design. As long ago as the 1970s, Porsche's racing department made its acquaintance with the heat dissipation problems created in a cylinder head with four valves per cylinder. The first step towards water cooling as a remedy was taken in 1985 on the Porsche 959, which had water-cooled cylinder heads with four valves per cylinder – but still retained air-cooled cylinder barrels. Porsche's more recent competition engines, however, confirm that the change to water cooling is an inexorable process.

**Peak power output and torque are just two Boxster target figures among many.**

In this case, however, project leader Kapfer and his designers were not content merely to produce a water-cooled version of the existing flat-six. They went all the way back to basic principles, which indeed are all that remain of the previous engine apart from the 116 millimeter spacing of the cylinders.

With the aim of creating a particularly solid foundation for high power output, the engineers introduced a revolutionary technique for the crankshaft's seven main bearings. They created a special aluminum bearing housing into which the steel bearing seats are cast. Securely encased in this way, the main bearings remain free of stressing and backlash, even under changing housing temperatures. Smoothness, refinement and above all long life are just a few of the many benefits.

**Each time a crash test is performed, one of the enormously expensive prototypes has to be sacrificed.**

This ingenious means of locating the main bearings in a separate bearing carrier has advantages too when the engine is being assembled because the bearing carrier can be inserted between the two halves of the engine block together with the fully assembled crankshaft drive (crankshaft, conrods and pistons) and bolted into position. Both the crankshaft and the conrods are steel forgings. The big end caps are produced by a remarkable modern method: after the joint line has been "scored out" by a laser beam, the cap is simply broken off by applying sufficient force. The crystalline structure of the break creates two perfectly matching contact surfaces, so that the joint line is invisible when the big end expansion bolts have been tightened.

Under the crankshaft, in the bearing carrier, there is a countershaft driven by a chain at a ratio of 2:1. From this shaft, two further chains run to the exhaust camshafts, one on each bank of cylinders. The chains and their cases make use of the space created by the flat engine's offset cylinders. For this reason, one chain runs on the right on the clutch side to the cylinder head and transmits power to the camshaft on the left at the front of the engine. The second chain runs to the left cylinder head at the front of the engine. This clever arrangement keeps the complete engine as short as possible – an invaluable feature for a compact mid-engined car. Although the cylinders are at the same spacing as on the earlier air-cooled flat-six engine, the water-cooled Boxster unit is actually 58 millimeters shorter.

The engine block is split vertically down its centerline. Each half of the crankcase is cast as a single unit with three cylinders on each side. 8.25 liters of engine oil are provided for lubrication, in a chamber beneath the main bearing carrier. This is not a wet sump, although it is part of the main engine block, but an entirely separate oil supply system. Porsche's engineers therefore refer to it as an "integrated dry sump" system. To ensure that oil pressure cannot drop when the car is cornering fast, despite the absence of a separate external oil tank, the oil pump's suction pipe is surrounded by an oil collector with flap-type non-return valves. These trap a quantity of the return flow so that the pump is never starved of oil.

The engine block, as one would expect, is made of aluminum. In contrast to Porsche's water-cooled four- and eight-cylinder engines, however, an aluminum-silicon alloy is no longer used. The new "Lokasil" process developed by the specialist Kolbenschmidt company in nearby Neckarsulm enables the silicon to be concentrated in the areas where it is most needed. *Silicon is added to aluminum alloys in order to obtain a largely wear-free surface for the cylinder walls, but in the Lokasil process it is located in separate cylinder liners. These are placed in the molds used to cast the Boxster's engine block, and incorporated into the surrounding aluminum by a special low-pressure method known as "squeeze-in casting". Porsche is the first manufacturer to adopt this method, which has considerable production advantages: the aluminum itself is less brittle and can be more easily machined. The cutting tools last longer, and the surfaces of the Lokasil liners are of a higher quality than obtainable with any material previously used. Lower friction means in turn that wear rates are reduced and fuel consumption is improved.*

The generous cylinder spacing of 118 millimeters between centers, the same value as on the previous opposed-cylinder engine, enables the open-deck design principle to be used, with the water surrounding the cylinder liners completely for efficient cooling.

The cooling circuit is based on the cumulative experience that Porsche has acquired in all areas of motor-vehicle engine design, notably the high-performance TAG racing engines. These 1.5-liter six-cylinder units, which collected three world championship titles, were capable of producing more than a thousand horsepower in practice trim on their best days. The same technology used to guarantee consistent temperatures around each cylinder and combustion chamber is now standard on the Boxster engine. The coolant flows vertically from the top to bottom of each cylinder bank. In the engine block the flow is divided by a metal gasket and passes round the cylinder head and cylinders separately. To ensure that the two sides of the horizontally-opposed engine receive equal flows of coolant, a distributor is flanged to the outside of the block. It contains the oil and water pump drives, so that heat exchange can take place between the water and oil flows. The complete circuit, with engine block, two radiators and the heater circuit, contains 17 liters of coolant, protected by an antifreeze additive.

A gear-type pump on the front of the engine maintains oil pressure to the various bearing points in the integrated dry sump circuit. When laying this out, the engineers strove to avoid external oil hoses and to use only internal oilways cast into the main elements of the engine. This not only keeps the design clean and tidy but has the additional real advantage of reducing the risk of leaks. For the same reason, the previous type of oil cooler is no longer used. Its place is taken by an oil-water heat exchanger flanged directly to the engine block. This improves warming up too, when a cold engine is started: the cooling water heats up more rapidly than the 8.25 liters engine oil at first, and thus helps to raise it to the regular operating temperature within a shorter time. Close examination of details of the Boxster's engine design also reveals two small auxiliary pumps, one in each cylinder head, to ensure the reliable return flow of the oil which collects in the lower part of the head.

The mid-engine's oil circuit is monitored by a sensor which transmits oil-level signals to a cockpit instrument. There is of course a dipstick as well, for manual checking of the oil level.

Thanks to their unconventional chain drive layout, the cylinder heads have the major advantage of being identical, so that they can be produced more efficiently. Other aspects of their design also reflect the state of the art: double overhead camshafts on each side of the engine, variable valve timing and four valves per cylinder. Yet the number of parts has been kept to a minimum and the heads are designed to permit the use of modern, efficient production methods.

A three-deck principle proved to be most suitable: the base is formed by the cylinder head itself, containing the combustion chambers and water passages. It accommodates a separate camshaft housing, complete with camshaft bearing pedestals, guides for the flat-base tappets and oilways. The top layer of the sandwich is a cover which also incorporates the bearing caps.

Porsche's engineers have provided a very simple but effective means of varying valve opening times at the inlet camshafts, in order to obtain a better torque curve. The small chain which links the two camshafts on each side of the engine passes round a tensioning element, which can be repositioned by an electric motor in response to signals from the Motronic engine management system. The four valves in each Boxster engine's combustion chamber are surprisingly small compared with the two in each cylinder of the 911 engine.

The inlet valves are 33.3, the exhaust valves 28.1 and the valve stems a mere six millimeters in diameter. A single taper-wound valve spring is all that is needed to close each valve reliably. The flat-base tappets incorporate hydraulic valve clearance adjusters. An air intake manifold made of plastic material supplies air from the central throttle butterfly through ducts with extremely smooth walls to the inlet valves. Electronic fuel injection operates sequentially, each cylinder having its own injector in the inlet port.

Electronic engine management from the Bosch company controls the injected fuel volume and the correct injection timing, and ensures that the engine idles at a stable speed. The Motronic computer also controls ignition timing and spark distribution, and responds to signals from the cylinder-selective knock control system. As would be expected today, the Boxster engine features solid-state high-tension ignition distribution, with a separate coil for each cylinder integrated into the spark plug cap. A special feature aimed at enhancing environmental friendliness is the air feed to the flange of the stainless-steel tubular exhaust manifold. This secondary air injection principle has a post-oxidizing effect which speeds up purification of the exhaust gas. A "stereo" oxygen sensing system with an oxygen sensor and a catalytic converter on each side of the engine takes care of exhaust emission control. The Boxster engine's modern design with four valves per cylinder speeds up gas flow through the cylinders and enables high power to be obtained from a relatively small swept volume. This first representative of the new Porsche engine generation has a bore of 85 and a stroke of 72 millimeters, yielding an effective displacement of 2479 cc. At an engine speed of 6200 rpm, this short-stroke unit develops 204 bhp (150 kW). Its specific power output of 82.3 bhp per liter is distinctly higher than that of the 3.6-liter Carrera. The latest opposed-cylinder engine also leads the way in torque, with 245 Newton-meters at 5000 rpm, equivalent to a most impressive mean working pressure of 12.3 bar. Although the current Carrera engine produces more torque, thanks to its displacement of 3.6 liters, its mean working pressure of 11.9 bar is lower, though still excellent for a two-valve engine.

**Crash simulation on the computer is often a way of determining where additional strength is needed without destroying valuable material.**

When looking for a suitable transmission to match their new engine, Porsche's technical people were able to avoid the classic route by way of drawing board and computer screen, and select a unit suitable for their chosen "lean production" methods. A five-speed gearbox, perfectly matched to the Boxster's power output and torque, was obtained at moderate cost from one of Porsche's long-established suppliers. The Tiptronic S automatic transmission too, which has five speeds now to suit the Boxster's engine characteristic, was of course available off the shelf from the transmission supplier.

Intelligent design methods and the brilliant combination of parts and assemblies have enabled the young Boxster team to produce a power train at only moderate effort and expense which satisfies the most demanding technical standards. This was not just a question of saving money: the total number of parts has been significantly reduced as well. Despite having four valves per cylinder, the new engine consists of only 408 individual parts, compared with 480 parts in the "classic" two-valve engine which powers the 911.

CLAUSPETER BECKER

Previous page: Like all current Porsche models, the Boxster's sheet steel bodyshell is galvanized on both sides – the ideal form of rust protection that can last for whole decades according to current experience.

This page: Computer-controlled automatic welding on a new production line in Zuffenhausen guarantees cost-effective, high-quality assembly of the Boxster bodyshell.

Next page: The welding booths are populated entirely by robots these days! Without human intervention, they produce the several thousand spot welds that give the Boxster's body its exceptional strength.

Like every Porsche engine until now, each six-cylinder unit for the Boxster is completely assembled by a single, small team. Afterwards, it is rig-tested to check that it achieves the specified performance data.

Next double page: The Porsche Boxster is built up from pre-assembled modules on the final assembly line. The doors, for instance, arrive complete with glass, window lifters, locks and mirrors.

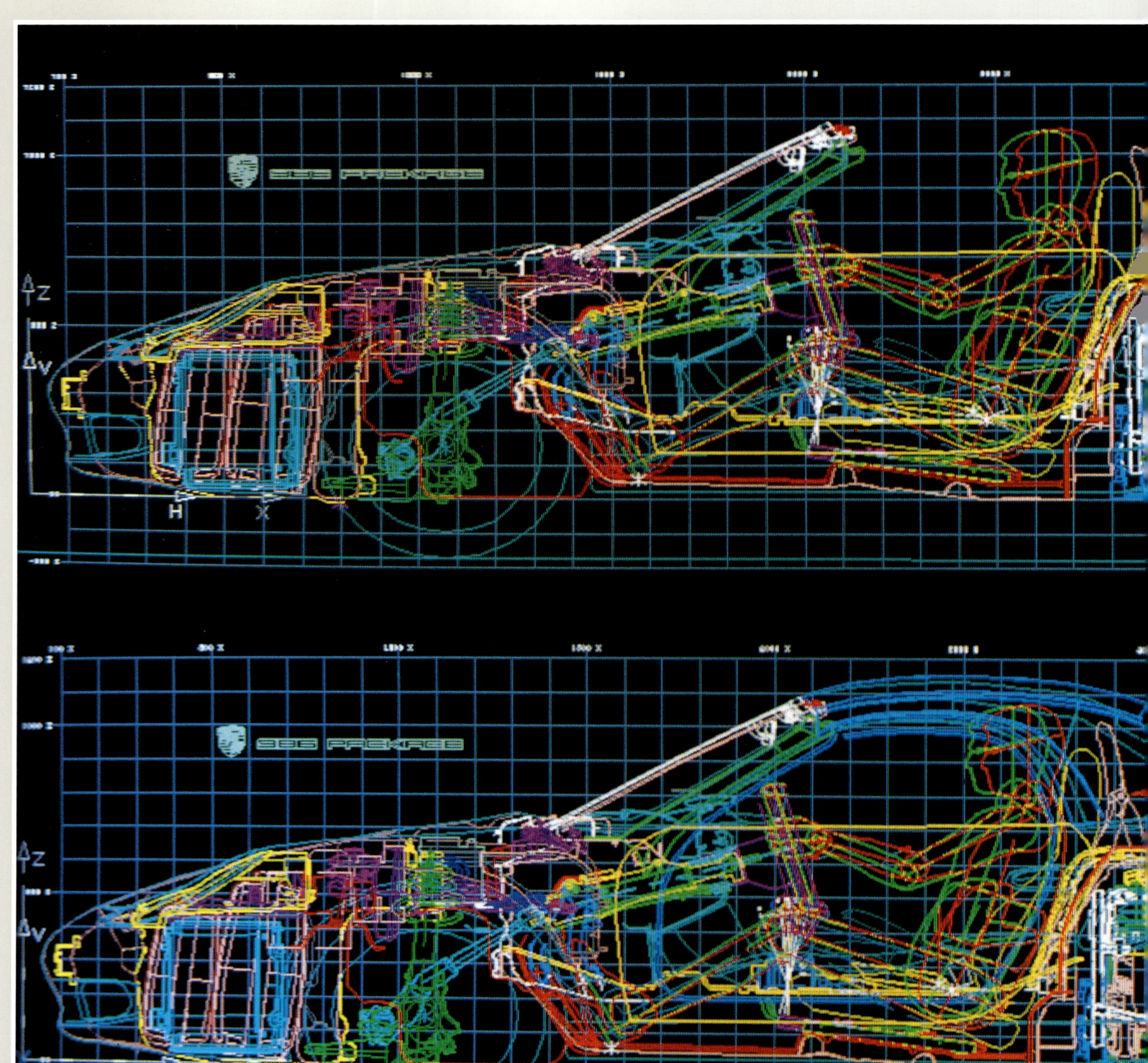

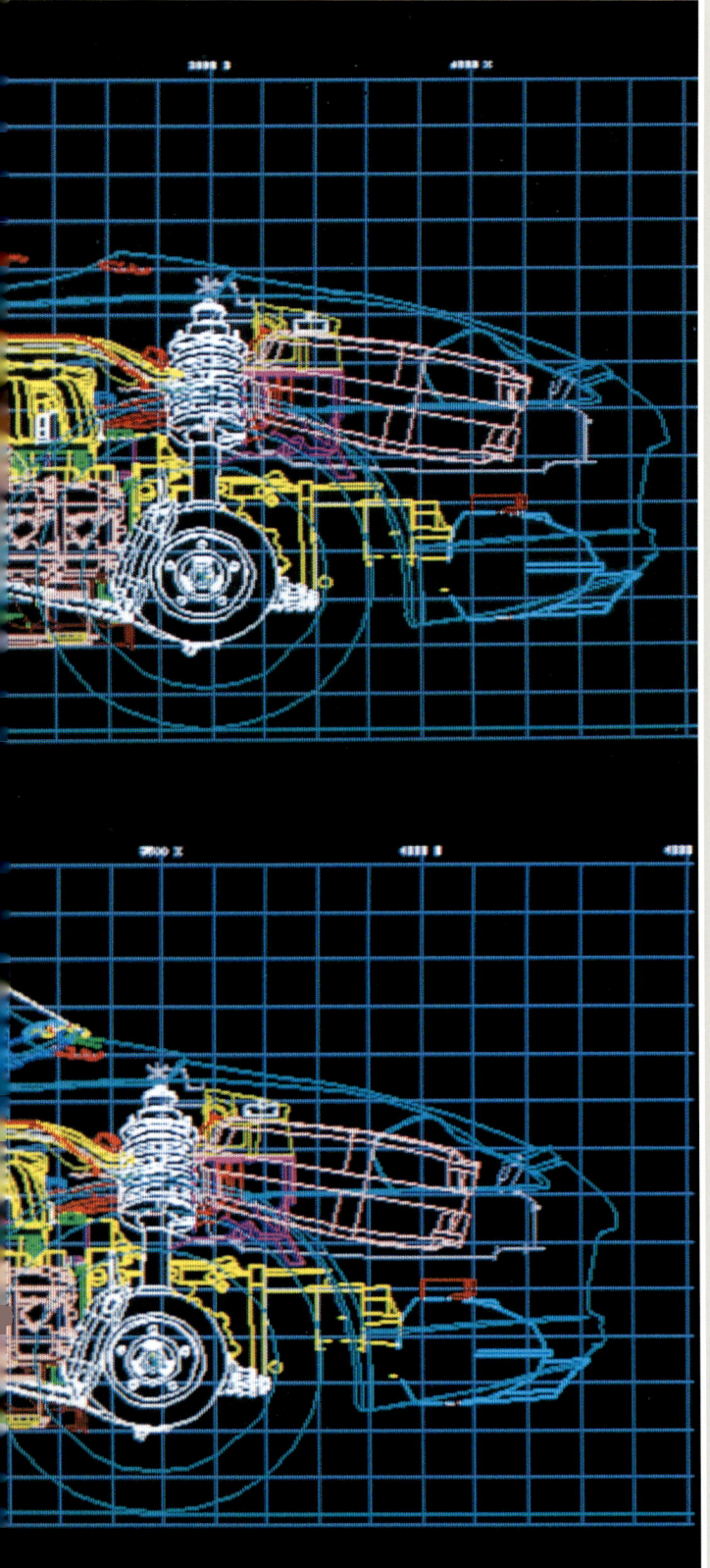
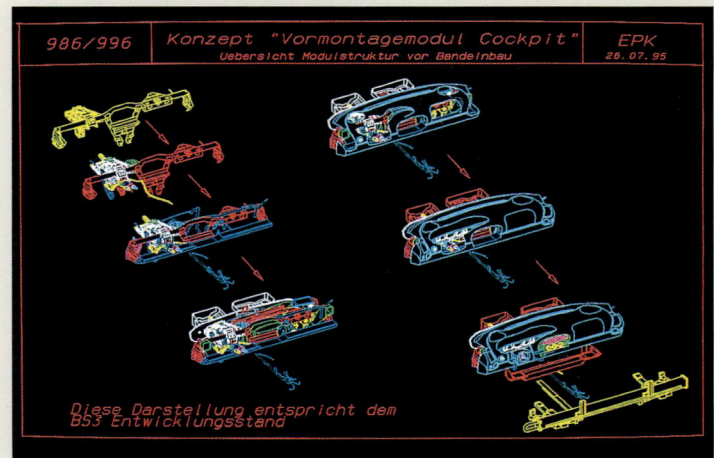
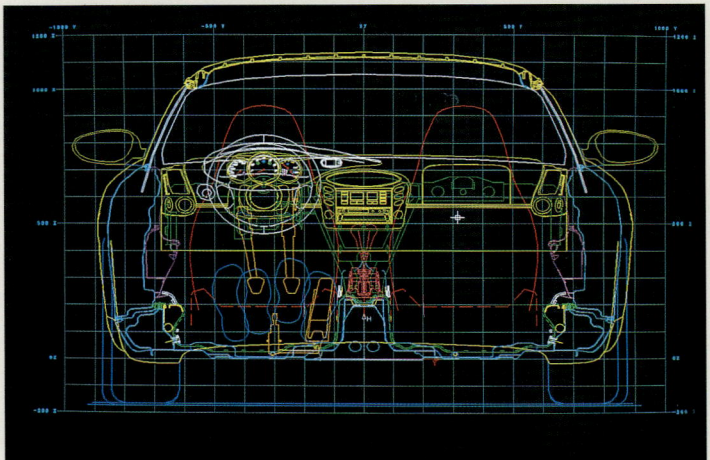

At the start of its development the Boxster, like every new car, was drafted out as a full-scale package drawing showing all the principal dimensions.

The Boxster is the first Porsche to adopt the latest principle of assembly from large, complex modular elements. But working conditions in the factory are not like those shown here in the photo studio!

# Accomplishing the Impossible

For the people who work at the Development Center in Weissach, creating the Boxster involved adopting modern and much more effective design principles for the first time: the buzzword for this is "Simultaneous Engineering".

At Porsche the future had already begun in 1992. The items that were on the wish-list for the still-young Boxster just could not be achieved by conventional automobile industry methods. The technical people were demanding a Porsche among the roadsters with a horizontally opposed six-cylinder engine of a totally new kind, combined with a perfect chassis and a convertible-quality soft top. The business people from Marketing were demanding an affordable Porsche to attract young buyers to the marque on an early rung of the social ladder, thus creating the potential for significantly increased sales figures.

Despite these seemingly irreconcilable differences, the Boxster team was able to agree at an early point on an almost shamelessly ambitious target: the car would not be an "economy Porsche", even if it did cost a lot less.

Thus the Boxster that emerged from the concept stage was not only close to the 911 from a technical standpoint, but considering the format of the 986 and its presumed weight of almost 1200 kilograms it was also obvious that there was not going to be much difference between it and its big brother. No matter how much the engineers and business people twisted and turned the number 986, the result was always the same: their mission was to make a car that by all conventional standards was impossible to make – a roadster at half the price of a Carrera convertible.

But the Boxster team in Weissach took this "mission impossible" as a perfect challenge for simultaneous engineering. Looking back on the now completed project, overall project manager Rainer Srock explains it this way: "We applied this new method of planning, developing, and making cars with a consistency that has never been seen before in the automobile industry."

Just like all ingenious ideas and processes meant to save time and money, simultaneous engineering works very simply: from the first day of planning the car is created by a complete team. The designers work right next to people who, in the past, were not consulted until much later. The production experts and their advice are integrated into the design process. They can say very early on whether a part can be produced efficiently and inexpensively, and how. A colleague from the purchasing department is also an active member of the team. He knows which suppliers could be used and which of them can even take over development work on individual parts or modules. When working according to this method, the production experts can make timely suggestions on how everything can be put together quickly and easily.

Development manager Ulrich Schempp describes this first try at simultaneous engineering as "... a far from easy learning process!" Today, the data sheet and price lists confirm that the seemingly impossible specifications were reached, and at the end the calculations even included some leeway for an electric soft top, a luxury not included in the original plans.

The first pilot run on the assembly line. In regular production conditions, of course, far fewer people are involved in assembling each Boxster.

The Boxster concept changed a number of things in the way cars, even Porsches, are built. The production process is an example of unexpected partnerships between competitors. Body parts, for example, are made by BMW at its press plants in Dingolfing, Eisenach and Munich.

The fabric soft-top with its magnesium linkage is supplied by Car Top Systems in nearby Münchingen, which Porsche operates jointly with Mercedes. The first use of cast magnesium for the soft-top linkage has already received world-wide acclaim. At a convention in Ube (Japan) the International Magnesium Agency awarded the Porsche design first prize, even before the first customer had the pleasure of using this easy-to-operate roof.

For the Boxster, traditional suppliers were contracted for larger delivery volumes. The Krupp-Hoesch group not only delivers the Bilstein suspension struts, but also the most important parts of the front and rear axles. Besides producing the disc brakes, Brembo in Cumo (Italy) also supplies the wheel carriers.

Production of the Boxster, in which modern modular technology plays a major role, requires only about half the number of hours needed to produce a Carrera. The fact that rationalization and high technological standards are not mutually exclusive is proven by even minor details of the Boxster's body. Its exemplary torsion-resistant structure despite its open design, and its high degree of passive safety in a crash are the result of consistent exploitation of the ideal qualities that steel, the classic material, offers to the automobile designer.

The front of the car, with the luggage compartment in the middle and the two radiators at the sides, provides a programmed crumple zone should the worst happen. The forces that are set into action here in a crash are diminished by the generous amount of deformation travel, leaving relatively little energy to reach the car's occupants. In the event of a rear-end collision, essentially similar design features at the rear of the Boxster ensure exemplary low risks of occupant injury. Another part of the Boxster's comprehensive safety concept is effective protection in the event of a rollover accident. The two roll bars of steel tube construction are only the visible part of the care that Porsche takes in safety matters. The second, invisible portion of the preventive measures is hidden, and takes the form of highly rigid steel tubing in the windshield frame.

The two airbags are of course also part of the Boxster's comprehensive safety package, and in the worst scenario, they are currently one step ahead of the rest. Their rescuing gas inflation comes from new azide-free gas generators that use an organic propellant. The advantages of the new technology are lower weight and the fact that these airbags are much easier to produce and, at some later stage, easier to recycle.

Given the fixed target of absolute strength and torsional rigidity at reasonable weight, sheet metal and tubing of 27 different special grades are employed in the Boxster. The term "tailor-made" would not be out of place here, and it is even used in the name of the "tailored planks", that is to say metal sheets that change their thickness at various points so that they can absorb different forces. Another of the specialties of modern lightweight sheet metal construction is wave-like panel edge trimming that has projecting tongues only where there will be welding points.

According to special project manager Horst Petri, the use of traditional steel in body construction has more going for it than just low production costs. "Sheet-steel bodies can be repaired relatively easily – all over the world."

As the Boxster went from design study to series production, a certain amount of growth was to be seen in the body area, which finally stretched it out beyond the dimensions of the 911. According to Ulrich Schempp, the reason for this was the "obligation to fulfill the target specification."

"Since we wanted to sell the Boxster as genuine business and travel car and not just as a toy," he adds, "the second luggage compartment was necessary in order to ensure a generous amount of space."

T his ambitious target was attainable only with a considerable amount of effort. There are two radiators in the nose of the Boxster, which keep out of the luggage compartment's way by making use of space in the fenders at each side.

When it came to the Boxster's soft top, the designers took the plunge and re-invented the convertible. This is the first fabric roof to depart from the tradition of the coachbuilding era of simply folding the cloth and linkage backwards to make it small enough to be stowed away. The Boxster's roof is totally different: it folds itself flat in a Z-shape pattern in its space under the lid, with the outside remaining on top to protect the underside from getting dirty.

During testing it became evident that the folding procedure for this soft top with magnesium linkage could be performed quite easily by a small electric motor. And as the cost-benefit analysts duly noted, women drivers in particular will thank Porsche for providing an electric soft top as standard equipment. There is not much more to do when you open the roof than to release a central safety lock and press a button. Twelve seconds later the soft top has disappeared into a compartment in the car's smooth tail. Afterwards a wind deflector can be mounted to protect that freshly blow-dried hairstyle.

**The soft top and its cover are opened and closed by electric motor.**

The complete roof assembly is supplied to the final assembly line "just in time" and ready to instal.

The chassis concept for the new mid-engined Porsche 986 is not just different from the 911 because the latter has a rear engine; the engineers also chose a different form of suspension that meet the needs of the Boxster in a variety of ways. The front and rear axles both use the McPherson principle with suspension struts and a lower wishbone. First of all this saves a tremendous amount of space that makes it easier to accommodate a worthwhile luggage compartment up front, as well as fitting well into the confined space close to the mid-engine at the rear. The design, which uses a large number of identical parts, simplifies production and cuts costs. And since it is a module supplied complete by another company, it corresponds with the efforts being made to keep production costs down.

The dynamic driving qualities of this rational design flowered to maturity in Weissach to the great satisfaction of the developers, who have more than thirty years of 911 experience behind them in designing front axles of this type. The front half of the development process was therefore a successful continuation of routine work. When designing the rear axle, the engineers used track rods to achieve the same toe-angle correction when cornering that had already given the so-called "Weissach axle" on the Porsche 928 its stabilizing effect.

"The excellent mass distribution of a mid-engine car definitely made our job easier," says chassis expert Peter Hentschel. The advantages of a consistent racing car concept are ideal for the roadster. Concentration of mass in the center of the vehicle improves handling and enables the car to be turned responsively into bends. The secret of setting up the suspension on this type of production automobile is to keep the car's willingness to change direction within safe limits, so that the over-ambitious driver cannot spin the car too easily. The key to doing this lies in the perfect matching of all components, starting with the steering and ending with the tires.

The modern lightness of driving calls – even on a distant descendant of the Porsche Spyder 550 – for power steering that is matched to the total weight of 1250 kilograms. Although the test drivers felt that the Boxster was agile, effortless and a pleasure to drive on twisting roads even without power steering, one should never forget that every journey starts and ends with parking the car, so that even the young and athletic roadster enthusiast will welcome the presence of this modern hydraulic system.

When it comes to braking, Porsche has often called upon the services of the Italian Brembo company. For the Boxster, four ventilated disc brakes with diameters of 298 and 292 millimeters were chosen, a sure sign that there have been no economies in the wrong area. Fixed calipers with four pistons at the front and two at the rear, and of course ABS, once again confirm Porsche policy that the engine's performance must always be matched by a similarly high level of braking power.

CLAUSPETER BECKER

On the way to the summit – Porsche importers were taken to the Jungfraujoch near Interlaken, Switzerland on March 4th, 1996, and given a first glimpse of the Boxster.

Porsche's chief executive Dr. Wendelin Wiedeking breaks down a wall of snow to reveal the Boxster nestling inside a giant igloo.

An unusual setting for an unusual presentation – has a new car ever before been put on display at an altitude of 3,500 meters and a temperature of minus 28 degrees?

# Porsche on Ice

How to convince Porsche importers from all over the world that the Boxster will bring them untold pleasure? Easy: fly the car up to 3,500 meters above sea level, hide it away in an igloo at 28 degrees below zero – and see what comes to light!

Seen close-up, it was unsurpassed dramatic theater. The audience at this event ran to more than a hundred people, carefully selected as participants in a spectacle of a very special kind. This private party witnessed a "peak performance" in more sense than one …

"Porsche on Ice" might have been a good title for this event, with the Porsche company acting as the producers. At an altitude of 3,500 meters, with temperatures of minus 28 degrees Centigrade and occasional wind-speeds of a hundred kilometers an hour, Porsche importers from all over the world were invited to an unusual meeting.

For the traditional importers' meeting, held every year just prior to the Geneva Motor Show, Porsche had excelled itself in choosing an unusual location: a plateau near the Jungfraujoch pass in the Swiss mountains above Interlaken. Having bravely penetrated this icy wilderness, the invited guests from 44 countries found the Boxster waiting for them, literally "on ice", and were able to witness its awakening to life.

On March 4th, 1996 at 12.30 p.m., Porsche's chief executive Wendelin Wiedeking seized an axe and, with vigorous support from Sales Director Hans Riedel and Development Director Horst Marchart, uncovered the entrance to an underground ice cave. In the middle of this igloo, gleaming in its classic silver paint, stood – the new Porsche Boxster!

Well before its presentation to some 800 journalists from all around the world in September, the plan was to have this group of international importers witness the first flicker of the new baby's eyelashes, so to speak. And why not in the eternal snows of the Swiss mountains, since the Boxster was still top secret at the time – quite literally "on ice" for a few months more?

The valuable one-off automobile had been hoisted up to the Jungfraujoch shortly before by a freight helicopter and maneuvered across the snow into its icy igloo, there to await discovery by the intrepid team of importers.

Porsche customers around the world have already ordered some 10,000 Boxster sports cars from importers and Porsche Centers – without knowing the new car's precise specification or its exact price, and indeed without ever having set eyes on this splendid new roadster. Now, face to face with the "Boxster on the Rocks", the standing ovations from those who had placed these "blind" orders seemed never-ending.

Following the "Boxster Presentation Special", the guests present on this clear and sunny day were flown by helicopter back down to the warmer valley. For those attending its importers' meeting, Porsche chose a selection of classic forms of transport: exquisite panoramic cars from the Swiss railroad, horsedrawn coaches, old-timer buses, cog railways, helicopters and even old DC-3 airplanes to conquer the distances and altitudes between the individual sites where its highlights were being presented.

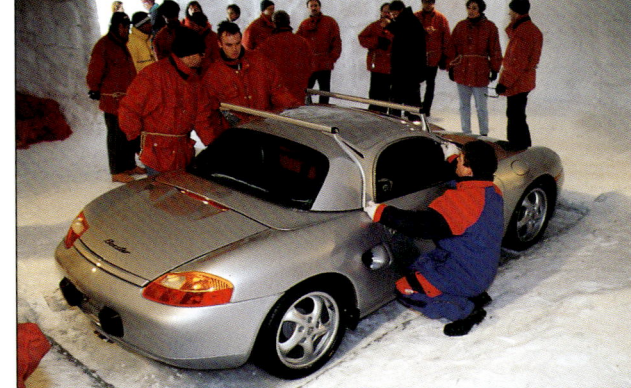

**The standing ovations knew no end – Porsche's importers were delighted by what they saw.**

On the day after this unusual "Boxster Summit", the importers visited the Geneva Motor Show. Those who flew in from Interlaken were like the holders of a state secret. What had been revealed to them – as if by some miracle – less than 24 hours previously amid the snow and ice, and what they had been able to examine and touch, was nowhere to be seen at the automobile industry's traditional spring gathering beside Lake Geneva, except in photos – the Boxster!

Ready for all weathers: thanks to its ingenious soft top, the Porsche Boxster transforms itself from "closed" to "open" in just a few seconds. There is also a hardtop to convert it into a coupé that's proof against the worst rain, snow and storms.

Whenever a new Porsche appears, it attracts the interest of technical enthusiasts and connoisseurs of automobile beauty. These firefighters were no exception – they surrounded and took possession of the Boxster. Soon, only the veriest hermit will not have heard of it …

# Advertising – an Essential Ingredient

One could of course deliver new cars and simply wait and see what happens. Porsche adopted a different approach: one of the most elaborate dealer presentations of all time. The motto: if you've built something good, why not tell the world?

All those who have already lost their heart to a creation from the works in Zuffenhausen, may be tempted to ask why Porsche had to dream up a large-scale advertising campaign for the new Boxster, why the Press Department planned the biggest presentation in the company's history and why dealers from all over the world were invited to Arizona for the launch event.

Wasn't it enough in January 1993 for potential Porsche customers to read in the "Cars" column of their daily papers or in the "News" section of their favorite car magazine that Porsche had exhibited a small and extremely attractive roadster design study at the Detroit Motor Show? A design study that attracted just about everyone's attention? And wasn't the Boxster in any case the first entirely new Porsche model since the 928? Surely all this would arouse the interest of potential Boxster buyers sufficiently, after a few first-drive reports in the big dailies and car magazines, to send them flocking down to their dealers?

"If only it were as easy as that!" says Gerd E. Mäuser, Head of Central Marketing at Porsche. "The first appearance of a totally new model has to take place long before the customers have a chance to sit in it at their Porsche dealers." Anton Hunger, Head of Porsche's PR department, agrees: "Only if the public knows early enough that a new model is on the way will it resist the temptation to buy from competitors and wait for the car it wants to appear."

Back in Detroit, the birth of the Boxster began in the winter snow when car journalists enthused over the Boxster design study, setting off an avalanche of emotions among their readers. A successful blend of nineteen-fifties nostalgia and contemporary style was what they saw, though something of a rough diamond still at this early stage. The first design study was of course too new to comply with all the constraints of volume production and the requirements of worldwide automobile legislation. But its captivating appearance and its technical specification were clear evidence of the direction which the Porsche company planned to take as the next millennium approached.

Most people have heard or read about the crisis that faced Porsche in the early 1990s. It was caused by a number of factors – economic recession in major markets, problems created by foreign exchange rate fluctuations and the company's remarkably large product range with three model lines and three entirely different engine concepts. The writing was clearly on the wall for the four and eight-cylinder model lines, though the classic 911 was never in any danger. This left a crucial question open: what form should the future of this renowned sports car manufacturer take?

Some intensive thinking began, with a few conclusions becoming obvious immediately: Porsche would have to be supported by two product lines in the future, since relying on a single model could prove disastrous. For reasons of cost, however, the new Porsche generation would obviously have to share a number of its parts with the 911 – and be offered for sale in a much lower price group. In view of the numbers of cars sold at  the 911's rarefied level, to introduce a model even higher up the scale would have been verging on the absurd. Last but not least, the new car would have to make a totally different impression than the 911, the aim being to produce a small but harmonious family of cars, not two deadly rivals within the same family.

After all this hard thinking there was really no longer any doubt about what the new car would look like: a small, easy to handle roadster with mid-engine, something to make the hearts of younger, leisure-oriented sports car fans in particular beat faster – a car to fully justify Porsche's claim to be an "Excitement Company". Introducing the Boxster was clearly the greatest challenge and opportunity ever to face the company, or as Gerd E. Mäuser puts it: "No other car in Porsche's history can claim to reflect so perfectly the changes and trends on today's automobile market. With the Boxster, Porsche is offering a car that ideally meets the needs and wishes of a younger customer group and its new consumer habits."

But how to set about convincing this essential group of potential customers that the Boxster was not only a very special Porsche but also something quite out of the ordinary on a roadster market that was already beginning to expand rapidly? Anton Hunger welcomes the fact that so many manufacturers have launched new roadsters and convertibles recently: "Every new model is an advertisement for a market segment that is still fairly small. Since the soft-top revival a year or two ago, customers are taking a fresh interest in this most attractive form of driving after having put the idea out of their minds for many years."

Although the Boxster had distinguished ancestors in the form of Porsche Number One, no less, and the successful "550 Spyder", it faced the problem of possessing no immediate precursor in the company's model range. And as we know, every new car starts to age the moment the public sets eyes on it. "It's true to say that a car's production cycle starts when the public sees it for the first time," says Gerd E. Mäuser. He knew that after having been previewed in Detroit, the Boxster would have to be put back under wraps as quickly as possible. "Our job was to make the new car rare and desirable. We wanted potential customers to struggle to remember what they had seen. We aimed to make the Boxster a legend before its time – a car that people would talk about before it went on sale, although they had no exact picture of what interested them so much."

**The aim was clear from the start – the Boxster was to become a legend in its time – and attract younger customers to Porsche**

Although three and a half years is a relatively short development period for a totally new car, this period seemed a lot longer to the members of Porsche's Marketing and Press departments. In the first few months, the "Boxster legend" was nourished by memories of Detroit and speculation as to whether the car would actually be produced. Slowly but surely, the Press department withdrew from all forms of discussion on this topic, and did not distribute any press photos of the design study either. The car magazines therefore took over the task of speculating on the Boxster's future and its technical details – with varying degrees of success. Among potential buyers, however, there was a steadily growing desire for more information.

It was not until the German Motor Show (the "IAA"), held in Frankfurt during September 1995, that the first press advertisement for the Porsche Boxster appeared – but the public still had to wait for its first glimpse of the car in its final form! A series of ads entitled "Boxster News" was then launched, to stimulate active interest in the car, though avoiding any clear indication as to its appearance. Not until March 1996 at the Geneva Car Show was the Press Department prepared to issue the first official photo of the Boxster. It was surely a sign of the keen public interest that the car depicted more often than any other in the media reports was one that was not even on show in Geneva!

The basic elements of this meticulously planned appearance had, however, been defined in an initial communication concept some years previously. This concept was subsequently revised and refined in several stages to produce a plan of campaign for a new Porsche company with its sales effort supported by two product lines. "It was both an advantage and a drawback that the Boxster had no predecessor in our model range," the company's Head of Marketing recalls. "On the one hand, this gave us a chance to create a new legend, but on the other, there was no direct means of relating the Boxster to our successes of the past." This comment naturally has to be taken with a pinch of salt, since Porsche's tradition most definitely includes a number of absolute highlights as reference vehicles for the design team under Harm Lagaay.

When a company finally decides on the direction it wants to take with its new model line, it is time for the marketing specialists to get down to work. Their task is to establish whether the target segment of the market has sufficient volume to absorb new models. The surveys carried out revealed that the convertible and roadster segment was likely to expand considerably throughout the world. More detailed analysis in fact suggested that the roadster market will enjoy above-average growth. Incidentally, Porsche was not the only company to arrive at this conclusion, as the steady stream of new roadster models since 1995 confirms.

So much for the quantitative side of the picture, but the market surveys naturally look closely at the qualitative side too, and analyze markets and potential customers all over the world in great detail. Here too, ample evidence in favor of entering the roadster segment was found, for example the trend away from mass-produced items towards "market niche" products, the high level of market saturation already reached in the leading industrial countries of the world and the implication that sales can therefore scarcely increase in total volume and must therefore be secured by qualitative measures. A look at the potential purchasers makes this clear: more and more of them pursue a lifestyle and plan their decisions with a view to achieving personal fulfillment. The products offered to them have to assist them in satisfying this increasing desire for individuality. There is no longer any clash of interests if someone snatches a quick bite to eat from a hot-dog stand at lunch time, and dines in a high-class restaurant the same evening. Another important marketing factor is the fact that the desire for new and exciting experiences remains as strong as ever.

There is no doubt about it: both markets and the public's consumption habits are becoming more and more individual. Since we live in a society which normally satisfies all our basic needs, we now have a chance to acknowledge a desire for

Having no direct predecessor was an advantage and a drawback at the same time: it was a chance to create a new, shining star, but without the firm foundation of a car with a high existing reputation.

stimulation of the senses, for self-fulfillment and for experiences of the more emotional kind. Consumers may indeed be paying closer attention to true value for money in their day-to-day purchases, but at the same time many of them have the financial reserves to buy articles which they believe will enhance their own lifestyle. This new trend in consumer behavior has divided markets into those for products which we need for our continued existence and well-being, and others for luxuries and articles associated with social status.

In recent years, our social behavior has in any case changed considerably. The central focus of our lives is shifting from work to leisure, the materialist view of the world is increasingly giving way to attitudes which have little or nothing to do with our working careers. We value ways of increasing the pleasure we gain from life more highly than the mere ability to collect and surround ourselves with material goods. Mobility becomes an experience in itself and part of the process of self-realization, well beyond the more mundane aspects of driving to work or using the car to go shopping.

The conclusions go still further: the important mainstays of the past such as product reliability, service, warranty and goodwill are slowly but surely becoming less important. There are two reasons for this: on the one hand, the pressure of competition is enormous, while, on the other hand, customers are better informed than ever before. Consequently, no company can risk exhibiting any weaknesses in these essential areas. Anton Hunger agrees: "It's fortunate that for Porsche, high quality was always a first essential." He recognized this trend early on: "Porsche has always concentrated on reliability, suitability for day-to-day use and the high resale value that these virtues imply. If this were not the case, the company would have found it difficult to survive as a pure sports car manufacturer."

"The average consumer doesn't exist any more," declares Gerd E. Mäuser, and in doing so speaks for the entire automobile trade. "The only typical feature of today's consumer is that he or she is unique! The new car-buying generation is on the lookout for individualized offers – and our Boxster is an ideal product for people who want to express themselves in this way."

Porsche always was a brand for the individualist, in fact there can be only a few other marques whose buyers differ so strongly from the mainstream. In appearance alone, a Porsche stands out in a crowd. In the words of Design Chief Harm Lagaay, the Boxster "suggests dynamism, with unusual forms and the ability to recall successful traditions. It's a new classic of its time, a modern bridge between traditional and contemporary aspects of design."

**There's no doubt about it: both the market and our habits as consumers are becoming more and more extreme**

With these five ads, Porsche aroused the interest of potential Boxster customers – although the new car is nowhere to be seen on any of them! A challenge to the readers' powers of imagination, stretching their curiosity to the limit before Porsche was ready to "lift the veil".

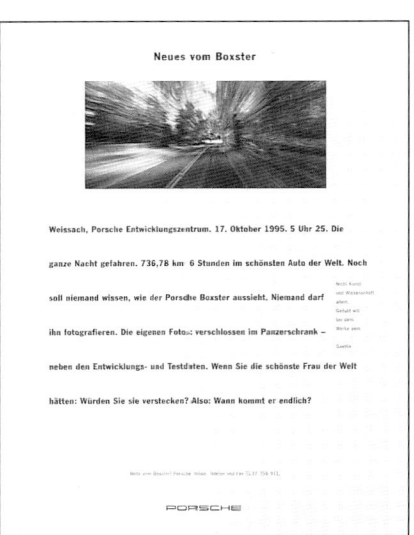

Many trends and findings therefore had to be taken into account in the early 1990s, when Porsche's future as a company was under close and serious scrutiny – new buyer groups ranging from young, high-income men and women, married couples with no children and two incomes through to the increasingly large group of older people whose children are now grown up and have left home, and who now intend to take up the active, experience-based life which they abandoned 25 years earlier for the sake of their children. Their world now centers far more on leisure than on work, with their hobbies and interests gaining in importance all the time. Such buyers have usually worked very hard for their money, and are not likely to spend it without careful thought. They want quality, not superficial glitter, and although their emotional urge to buy is strong, it has to be supported by rational arguments too.

We have already seen why the next Porsche generation almost had to be a small, easily handled open roadster. No model positioned above the 911 would have sold in sufficient numbers to pay for itself and restore the company's fortunes. The new car's technical specification therefore called for as many parts as possible to be shared with the 911, as a cost-saving measure and as a means of making servicing easier. The 911, however, had to preserve its unique status, which meant aiming the new car at an entirely different market segment. In other words, two product lines that complemented each other instead of representing a source of internal competition.

**Superficial design features are out these days – people will buy only if there are rational arguments in favor of the decision too**

It was therefore more than a happy coincidence that the youthful, sporty roadster market suddenly became the focus of attention again. The status of Porsche's latest model line benefits enormously from Porsche's reputation as the only manufacturer with a history of making nothing but sports cars. From the first Porsche in the late 1940s through the legendary 550 models and the successful racing cars, the engineering team in Zuffenhausen remained loyal to the mid-engine principle, with its outstanding traction and agility. Even the Porsche GT 1 that proved so successful in the 1996 Le Mans 24-hour race now has its engine ahead of the rear axle. The interesting thing about the Boxster in this respect is that the mid-engined concept creates space for two surprisingly large luggage compartments, one at the front and one at the back. Together with a highly versatile Roof Transport System, this will give the Boxster even more appeal in the eyes of its leisure-minded buyers. There is another close emotional link too between it and Porsche's range-topping 911 models: the six-cylinder engine, a sure sign that the family tradition is alive and well.

"A youthful, sporting model is obviously an opportunity to attract a new, more youthful public to the brand." Gerd E. Mäuser is confident that the Boxster will perform this task admirably: "Compared with the typical 911 owner, its buyers will be about ten years younger, earn about a third less and include about twice as many women." These are the kind of data that make the average sales manager jump for joy, since they imply a much longer period of loyalty to the marque and access to a hopefully satisfied group of potential customers for more expensive models at a later date. If more women choose the Boxster, this will benefit the marque in general too, by helping to eliminate some of Porsche's unjustified reputation as a manufacturer of "macho" cars.

"Younger customers mean that the Boxster will be run as the only car in the household much more often than the 911," Anton Hunger reminds us. And this was why great attention was paid during development to suitability for day-to-day use. "You can drive the Boxster 365 days a year. The soft top is effective, there is a hardtop option too, and the heater has been tested under arctic conditions so that snow and ice hold no terrors for it." As befits a car designed for practical use, the Boxster is equipped with body panels galvanized on both sides and full underbody paneling. All these measures help to ensure that it will keep its value the way a Porsche is expected to do.

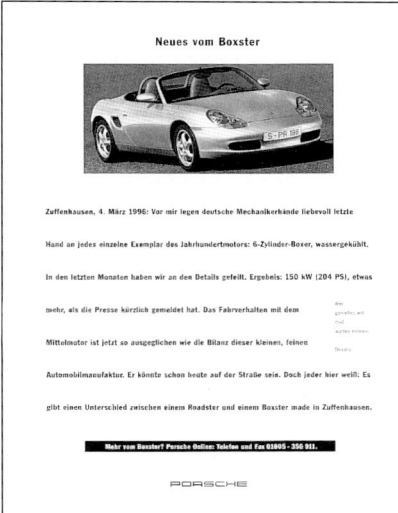

Marketing and press executives naturally took part in many of the meetings at Porsche's Weissach development center from the very outset. They were present at the "birth" of the new car, and by maintaining close contact with the technical people, helped to ensure that it matched Porsche's new image as an "Excitement Company". Internal discussions of this kind proved useful not only in maintaining Porsche's fundamental values such as tradition, originality and authenticity, but also as a means of pointing the Boxster in entirely new directions. Its styling, for instance, strikes a balance between a traditional, classic style and one containing youthful or even avant-garde elements. On top of this design quality came sporting character and dynamic handling, characteristics which customers have always identified with Porsche products. Then there is the sensual side, the sheer emotional delight of a car that looks so good and is also such fun to drive. To reach new, younger customer-groups, more down-to-earth objectives had to be kept in mind as well: moderate running costs and an acceptable purchase price – in other words the kind of genuine cost-benefit ratio to which Porsche has always been committed. In short, the Boxster is a highly attractive blend of the very latest technology, styling that echoes a great tradition and built-in practicality that makes the car ideal for day-to-day use. It is just the car that Porsche customers have been waiting for: a brilliant combination of traditional values and creative originality.

These two values – tradition and originality – are precisely those which Porsche's own workforce and its customers alike regard as the fundamental driving forces behind the company. Gerd E. Mäuser comments: "We realized from the start that the Boxster would one day play an important part in the tradition that gave rise to it. With its many remarkable innovations, for example the revolutionary roof system design, it will maintain Porsche's deserved reputation for creative and exciting automobile technology – which is already firmly established as a legend in itself!"

As the Boxster gradually developed from the very first sketches and models, the campaign to introduce it to a wider public also began to take on a definite shape. The public, as we all know, has its well-established pre-conceptions: advertising agencies, for example, are full of verbal acrobats who sit up all night with a pot of black coffee and appear, unshaven, clutching a sheaf of brilliant advertising copy. According to Gerd E. Mäuser, reality looks slightly different: "We initially define our advertising strategy in-house. It would be impossible for outsiders to decide how the company is expected to develop and which products we should sell. We have to keep control of strategy – but after this, we give the creative people a more or less free hand."

This explains why Klaus E. Küster, owner of the Frankfurt-based advertising agency of the same name, only received Mäuser's provisional marketing concept on November 23rd, 1994, together with market research data from the USA and an individual briefing on the subject of the Boxster. Küster recalls: "... but we never got to see the car! In December we bought a few models of the Boxster from Porsche, so that we could study its appearance and produce our layouts. We still didn't get a look at a real Boxster!" His ironic tale of woe continues: "By January 1995 I was in Bad Brückenau, the health resort, losing a pound in weight every day (Tao diet), going for two-hour runs and writing down, with my mind totally relaxed, my first 20 or 30 Boxster ideas. The client saw these on January 19th and was kind enough to give them a nod of approval. It was decided to run an interim campaign, to bridge the time gap before the actual Boxster became available. This campaign was called "Boxster News", and was approved on February 10th. But the car – you guessed it, we hadn't set eyes on it even by then!"

Two weeks later, Klaus E. Küster's ambition came true – he was granted an audience with a genuine flesh-and-blood Boxster. His response is typically acute and concise: "It inspires enthusiasm. The feeling is catching! Some of us, unfortunately, caught a cold too on this occasion." The next

A courtesy nod to Munich – Porsche's way of welcoming the launch of the BMW Z3.

**The advertising strategy is always defined in – house – and not by the advertising agency.**

**The first advertising ideas were developed after studying Boxster models – there were still no photos available**

meeting was on July 21st in Weissach, and this visit triggered the urgent desire at the agency to completely rethink the campaign. "We took the initiative and produced new motifs for the campaign that had already been agreed upon. The Boxster is a car that sets a whole lot of creativity free!" October 4th was to be the Big Day: "We presented a brand-new, totally revised campaign. The client preferred the old one – and I suppose he was right. That evening, we nevertheless drank a large quantity of beer."

On October 17th, 1995, which happens to be the 27th birthday of copywriter Sven Niemeyer, the first "Boxster News" advertisement was published, and Gerd E. Mäuser was able to draw a line under the first lengthy phase in the marketing operation. From that day on, advertising for the new model was officially in progress (though without it being pictured in the ads), and the countdown leading to the world première, the first press conference and the first deliveries to customers had begun. The ad copy was aimed at arousing curiosity, with the actual product nowhere to be seen. The Boxster was being held back as a trump card, to be played when the time was ripe. "Weissach, Porsche Development Center, October 17th, 1995. It is 5.25 in the morning. An all-night drive, 736.78 kilometers. 6 hours in the finest car in the world. In the dead of night, because we don't want anyone to know what the Porsche Boxster looks like. Or take its photograph. We have our own photos, of course – locked in the safe next to the development and test data. But if you were married to the world's most beautiful woman, you wouldn't want to hide her away, would you? So when can we tell the world?"

But the game of secrecy continued. In December 1995, the test team donned their winter jackets and took their computers and measuring equipment to the frozen north of Canada. In February 1996, they moved to Arjeplog in the north of Finland, to check the traction control system at temperatures 25 degrees below zero. In March, there were two new motifs: the first one contained a few polite sentences in response to the launch of BMW's Z3 model: "We welcome this roadster – made in the USA. And we sincerely hope you will wait for the Boxster – made in Zuffenhausen." Then came the Geneva Motor Show, and Porsche's press department issued the first official picture of the Boxster, which was now to be shown to a very much wider public.

The last ad before the big presentation to the media and the dealer launch emphasized once again that the Boxster was "Pure Porsche." The copy read: "Zuffenhausen, July 31st, 1996: the mid-engine is carefully installed by hand in a body which stole the show in Detroit four years ago and which triggered such a response that up a whole new market opened up. Of course, the high-volume automobile manufacturers cannot resist a trend like this, and they are bringing out one roadster after the other. Meanwhile, the true originators of the idea are pressing ahead unperturbed. We know that we are not building just any car. We are building a totally new type of car. From the first idea to the last nut and bolt. Pure Porsche."

"Of course, advertising alone is not enough today," says Gerd E. Mäuser. "That is why we started conducting mailing campaigns as well after the German Motor Show in 1995. In parallel with the ads, they provided potential customers with more information on the Boxster's new features. But we only sent the next episode to those who sent the reply cards back, as a sign that they were genuinely interested. This enabled us to collect data and study reactions, so that we were able to judge whether the prospect was likely to buy a Boxster later."

Media activities were of course coordinated closely with these marketing moves: "We also wanted to keep the tension high, and not make the Boxster too familiar to the public by releasing information early." But Anton Hunger was naturally also convinced from the very earliest planning stage that "we had to avoid letting too much time elapse between the presentation and the test drive reports in the media, and the Boxster's appearance in the dealers' showrooms."

Since a German car clearly has to be presented to the media on its own domestic market as well, the Press team chose the Schlosshotel Lerbach near the town of Bergisch Gladbach as the venue. A four-week presentation to a total of 800 journalists (250 of them from within Germany) began on August 23rd, 1996. Hunger's comment: "The longest and most elaborate press event that Porsche has ever held!" In the first two weeks, automobile journalists from Germany and other European countries visited this castle hotel in its romantic setting, followed later by groups from the USA, Japan and the rest of the world, not forgetting such far-away places as Australia, South Africa and New Zealand. "The effort was surely worthwhile for the first brand-new Porsche since the 928," says PR chief Hunger. "The Boxster is to be our company's second major product line, and we wanted all our markets to be fully informed about this at the same time."

Only three weeks later, it was time for about 500 dealers to be familiarized with the latest Porsche. In sunny Scottsdale, Arizona (USA) an event was staged for them, starting on September 11th, and attended by some 2,000 people on a series of four-day visits. Dealers, accompanied by their wives, enjoyed a welcome party and a static presentation first, to introduce them to the Boxster. After this, the whole many-sided "Porsche World" was on view in a specially built "village". This covered a variety of aspects of Porsche's technical prowess, tradition and heritage. Boxster Selection products were on display (fashion items, watches, spectacles etc.) and there was a special information stand to answer dealers' questions. Another stand that proved to be a great attraction was run by the Porsche Travel Club. This club offers adventure tours to destinations all over the world which dealers can sell to their customers.

At the end of this major event, dealers returned home freshly motivated and enthusiastic about what they had seen. Gerd E. Mäuser and Anton Hunger, meanwhile, were working on the final climax in the Boxster launch program: the official world première on October 1st, 1996 at the Paris Motor Show. At last, the "man and woman in the street" were able to see the Boxster in all its splendor. Even as the visitors crowded around it, the first demonstration cars were reaching dealers, the first test drives were being undertaken, the first sales were being concluded – and most important of all, the very first Boxsters were being delivered to their overjoyed owners.

The work was over, at least in the sense that the Boxster had been transformed so successfully from an idea into reality. Close study of market needs had resulted in an agile sports car capable of bridging every gap between tradition and the future, sense and sensibility, environmental awareness and sheer driving pleasure. But it was clear to all involved that this climax represented a new beginning: the start of the race for new customers and of the unceasing task of selling a true high-quality product. Porsche's marketing department certainly didn't plan to rest on its laurels: still under wraps but ready for immediate distribution were the posters, films, advertisements and leaflets for the next of many Boxster campaigns.

**A German car needs to be introduced in Germany too – 800 journalists accepted Porsche's invitation**

JÜRGEN LEWANDOWSKI

A great day in June 1948 – Ferry Porsche was able to show his father Ferdinand the now-famous "Porsche Number One", the first car to bear the family name.

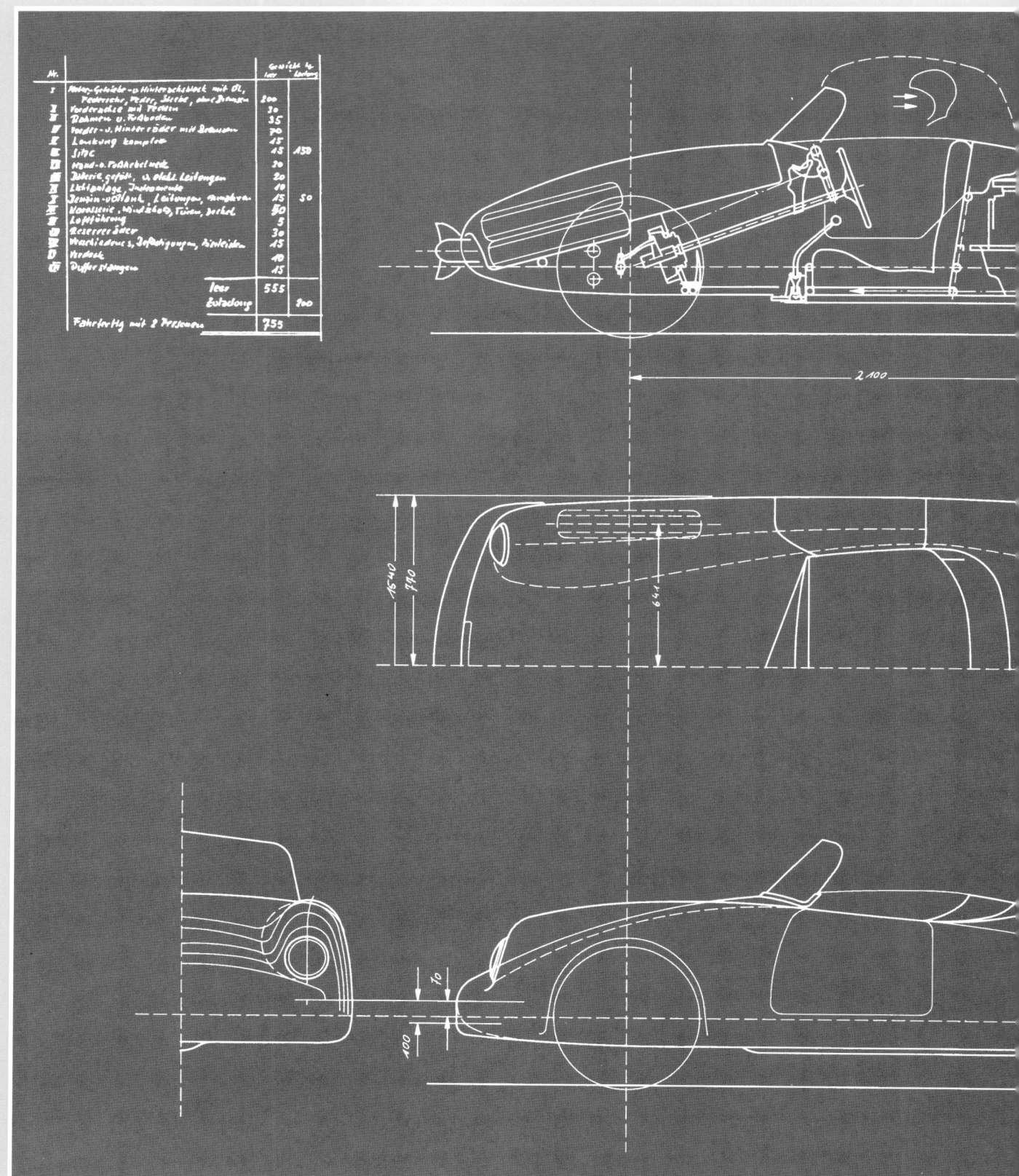

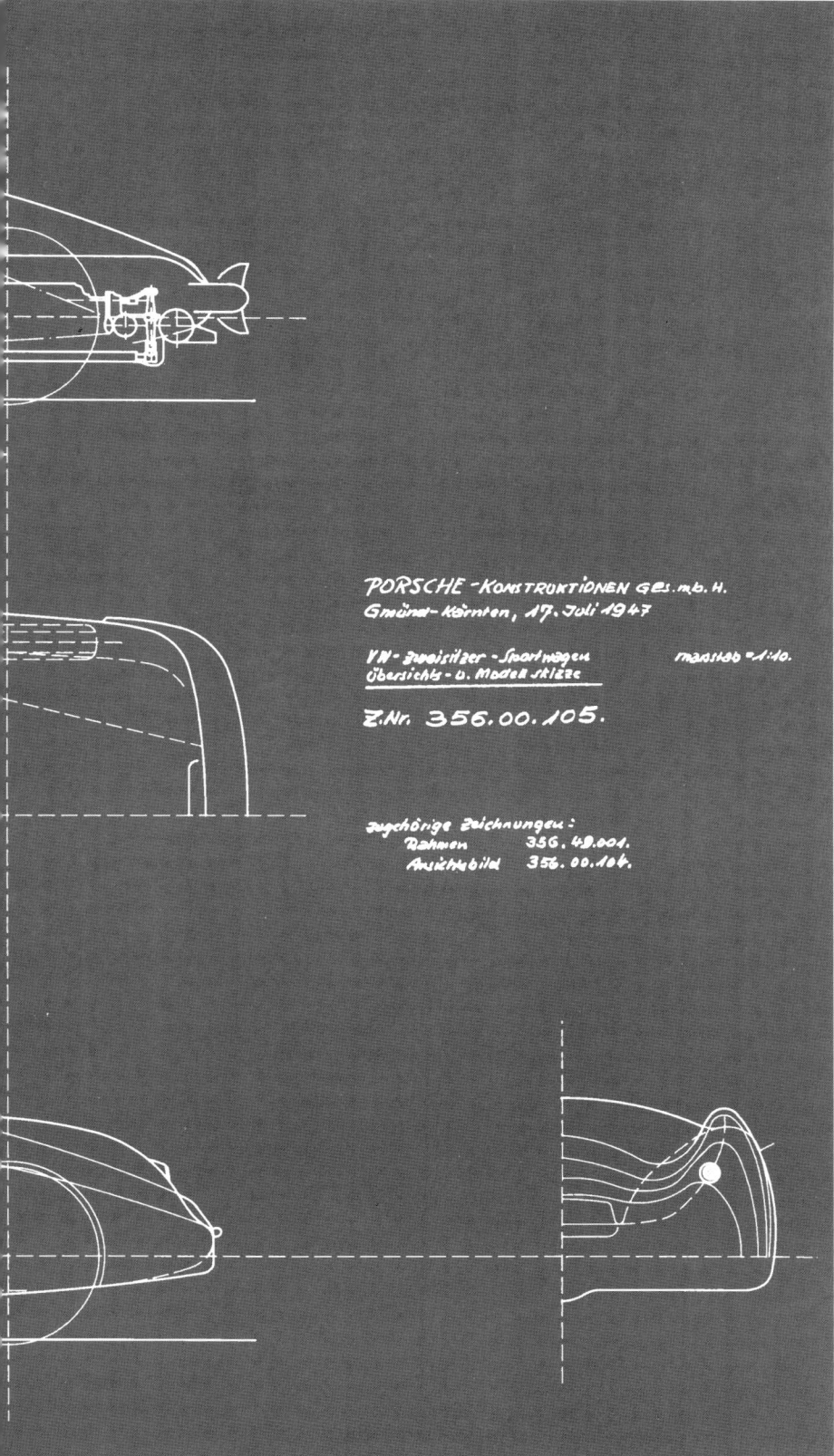

The beginning of a legend: the first drawing of a "two-seater VW sports car" dating from July 17, 1947, bearing design number 356.00.105. The weights are most carefully listed at the top left – even down to two spare wheels at 30 kilograms each.

Development of the 356 was based on the Porsche Type 60K10 of 1939, which was intended to take part in the subsequently canceled Berlin-Rome motor race.

James Dean – surely the most celebrated Porsche Spyder driver. He lost his life in a road accident when another driver failed to see his car and pulled out in front of him. His race mechanic Rolf Wütherich (left) survived, though severely injured.

The first two 550 Spyders ended up in Guatemala in 1953, bought by someone who was aiming for a class win in the Carrera Panamericana road race. Since then all trace of these cars has been lost.

An important moment for a still young company – the 550 Spyder was shown to the public for the first time at the Paris Motor Show on October 1, 1953.

# A Man and a Vision

The first-ever Porsche was mid-engined, and the first Spyder also had its engine ahead of the rear axle. A welcome opportunity for the latest sports-car generation to show that the old folk maybe knew a thing or two after all.

There can be very few automobile manufacturers whose archives or museums contain every detail of their products, from the first sketches and early drawings right through to the vehicle bearing chassis number 1. Porsche is one of these rare exceptions – the very first Porsche can be seen in the company's museum in Zuffenhausen, outside Stuttgart, and the corresponding documents and drawings are stored in the nearby company archives.

Obviously a new car doesn't come into being on its own – in fact it is nothing more than the practical realization of the ideas and thoughts of its creators. And these thoughts? They in turn are based on a vision. And it must have been a very powerful vision that took hold of Ferry Porsche and his team back in June 1948, when they produced their first two-seater sports car at their workshops in Gmünd, Austria, and attached the family name to it. Repercussions of the Second World War were still all too evident, and people were more interested in sheer transport capacity and movement from place to place than in concepts such as the "roadster" – a word that few of them had probably ever heard.

But Ferry Porsche had his vision, that of a comfortable sports car, and time was to prove him right. In view of the amount that has already been written about this particular automobile manufacturer, this is not the place to examine the whole development history of Porsche Number One. But there are a few interesting parallels which help to locate the Boxster accurately in Porsche's history, and give it the status it deserves. To do this, we have also taken a closer look at the Type 550 Spyder, various versions of which were built between 1953 and 1957.

Why do Porsche people at the headquarters in Zuffenhausen and at the development center in Weissach tend to regard these particular models as the legitimate forerunners of the Boxster? Well to start with, there are striking similarities between Number One, the 550 Spyder and the Boxster. All three are classic mid-engined cars, with the engine located just ahead of the rear axle. All three were designed as roadsters – and all three are shapely evidence that sound engineering design usually looks good as well. In his memoirs, Ferry Porsche writes: "We had plans to build our own car even before the Second World War broke out. Our development work was based on the Porsche Type 60K10, which was designed in 1939 to take part in the Berlin-Rome motor race, though this race was subsequently canceled." Instead, the new car with the project designation 356 was launched on June 11, 1947 at Porsche's premises in Gmünd, a town in the Austrian federal state of Carinthia. By July 17th, the first chassis drawings and the provisional body design had been completed. One of the most remarkable design features of the new sports car was without doubt its tubular space frame, produced by welding together sections of steel tube. This frame provided the extremely light car – the 356-001 weighed a modest 585 kilograms – with quite exceptional rigidity. A standard Volkswagen power unit was chosen. Ferry Porsche's comment: "We used parts that already had more than a million test kilometers behind them. We said to ourselves: 'If they stood up to years of tough treatment in Volkswagen's military vehicles, they ought to be just right for a sports car'."

However, as is usual at Porsche, the 1131 cc air-cooled opposed-cylinder engine was modified slightly to boost its power output: the valve diameters in the cylinder heads were enlarged and the compression ratio was increased from 5.8:1 to 7.0:1. Later, the original single carburetor was replaced by a twin-barrel unit – as a result the engine performance went up from the original 25 horsepower at 3300 rpm to 35 hp at an engine speed of 4000 rpm.

The great day arrived in March 1948: the first Porsche was started up and moved away, slowly at first, with Ferry Porsche at the wheel. The elegant body had not yet been fitted,

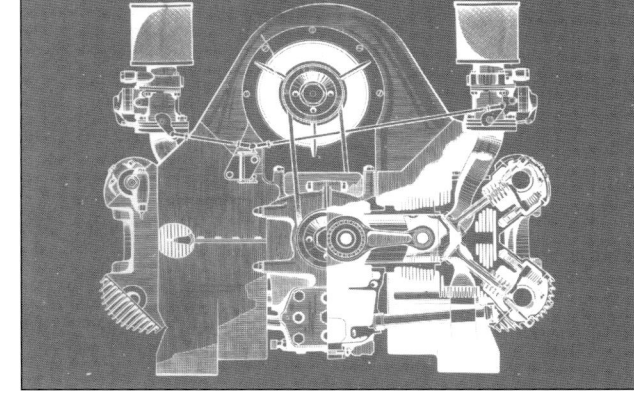

After this power unit appeared, things were different: the double overhead-camshaft unit designed by Ernst Fuhrmann developed 110 horse power on its very first outing.

**The first Le Mans entry on June 13th/14th, 1953: the 550 Spyder immediately notched up a double victory in its class.**

but without it "Number 001" was nonetheless taken up the nearby Katschberg Pass on its maiden journey. In April and May, the lightweight aluminum body so beloved of all Porsche enthusiasts was mounted on this first chassis. According to Ferry Porsche, "its aerodynamics were based on the know-how we acquired from the Berlin–Rome racing car". There are indeed certain similarities between the contours of the coupé racer built in 1939 and the post-war roadster: the nose, the headlights, the fenders and the way the rear end outline drops smoothly and gently away.

The 356, however, as launched in June 1948, was planned to be more of a well-appointed sports car than a competition vehicle. It had a comfortable, wide bench seat that could carry three people if the need arose. Its low weight, good aerodynamics, mid-engined layout, short wheelbase and rigid tubular frame combined to make "Number One" an exceptionally agile vehicle that, as Ferry Porsche puts it: "exceeded our expectations from the start. It climbed hills like a mountain goat and reached 130 kph on the road without the slightest difficulty." But at the same time, Porsche was fully aware of how much publicity could be obtained from motor racing, and only a month later, on July 11, 1948, his cousin Herbert Kaes, who was on the company's technical staff, drove Porsche Number One to an effortless class victory in a road race held in Innsbruck.

The next logical step was to plan for a small production run. Two Swiss businessmen, Rupprecht von Senger and Bernhard Blank, agreed to provide the necessary financial backing. Coupé and convertible models were also envisaged to accompany Porsche Number One. One thing was obvious, however, to all concerned: the elaborate tubular frame would be too expensive for series production, and in any case occupied too much valuable space in the vehicle.

This led to the construction of 356-2, with the engine relocated behind the rear axle in order to provide more passenger space, and a sheet-steel frame that was very much easier and cheaper to build. The new financial backers obligingly ordered the first five cars, whereupon production of the 356 commenced in Gmünd, and indeed fifty cars were built there before production was transferred to Stuttgart.

356-001 itself was sold to Rupprecht von Senger on September 7, 1948 for 7000 Swiss francs. Towards the end of the same year he also asked the company to build him a small trailer. This first Porsche changed hands in 1952, being purchased by Hermann Schulthess, who kept it until 1958 and then returned it to Porsche – where it is one of the highlights of the company museum to this very day.

It was 1953 before the next mid-engined Porsche left the company's constantly expanding production facilities. This was the Type 550 – the name Spyder was only added at a later date. Porsche purists will probably object that there were other mid-engined racing cars before the 550, built on the initiative of Frankfurt Porsche dealer Walter Glöckler. The first of these was built in the winter months of 1949/50, and by 1953 five cars had been produced, of such elegance and efficiency as to justify their displaying the Porsche badge. Glöckler often finished among the leaders in motor racing events with his vehicle, and carried off the German sports car championship at his first attempt in 1950. Not surprisingly, this attracted the attention of US Porsche importer Max Hoffmann, who had the second of Glöckler's cars shipped to the United States immediately and entered it for races there with much success.

In the late nineteen-forties and the early nineteen-fifties, Porsche did not have either the funds or the capacity to develop a pure competition car. It was not until 1953 that the first Porsche qualifying for this description saw the light of day: the 550. This open racing car had its world premiere on October 1, at the Paris Motor Show. At the time, nobody had yet applied the term Spyder to this mid-engined car with its lightweight aluminum body: it was to appear as a badge only in the fall of 1954, at the London Motor Show.

Wilhelm Hild, the Porsche engineer responsible for competition cars, had always been in close contact with Glöckler, and therefore (and no doubt because the budget was extremely tight) based his work closely on the car with which he was already familiar. It was more or less self-evident that the engine in a pure racing car would have to revert to its logical position ahead of the rear axle, and the company's ample experience with Grand Prix cars bore this out. The car's aerodynamics were good, its weight was low and the mid-engine concept made its handling extremely agile, but none of these advantages could be exploited fully until an engine of sufficient power became available.

In the spring of 1953, nobody outside Porsche's experimental department could know that Dr. Ernst Fuhrmann, later to become chairman of the Porsche board of management, had been busy since 1952 developing a four-camshaft engine. The young designer not only created a most unusual competition engine, but also one of the most successful ones of all time: known internally as the 547, it had an alloy block, and the cylinders and cylinder heads were also made of aluminum. The four overhead camshafts were driven by two vertical shafts. Since this was a pure competition engine, a twin-spark ignition system with two distributors and two coils was provided. Drawing its mixture in from Solex 40 PJJ twin-barrel downdraft carburetors, the engine developed 110 horsepower from a displacement of precisely 1498 cc, at an impressive 7800 rpm.

This was a time in which many mechanical assemblies were quite simply borrowed from series-production cars, so that the development period was relatively short. Only four months after design work had started, Porsche's competition manager Huschke von Hanstein was able to enter the first 550 for the Eifel race on the Nürburgring circuit in Germany. Tipping the scales at only 545 kilograms, it had a ladder-type welded steel tube frame with six cross-members. The front suspension, steering, brakes and wheels were taken from the production 356. The Frankfurt-based Weidenhausen coach-building company, which had also supplied bodies for the Glöckler Porsches, clad this weight-saving chassis and driveline in a neat aluminum body. The Fuhrmann engine was not yet ready to race at this time, and so a 1500 Super engine, running on alcohol, with a 12.5:1 compression ratio and a power output of just under 100 hp, was used instead.

On this 31st of May, a cold, damp day, the driver's seat of the first 550 was occupied by Helm Glöckler, a cousin of Walter Glöckler. Despite various problems with the carburetors, he scored an immediate victory on the car's first outing. Only a few weeks later came an even greater success: the two chassis bearing the numbers 1 and 2 achieved a convincing first-and-second class victory in the much-feared Le Mans 24-hour race, in the hands of the Richard von Frankenberg/Paul Frère and Hans Herrmann/Helm Glöckler teams. The engine with the double overhead camshaft heads then had its first official outing at the Schauinsland hillclimb, near Freiburg in south-west Germany. It had been installed and run unofficially earlier, during practice for the sports car race accompanying the German Grand Prix on August 2, but nobody had noticed at the time.

The first two 550s to be built were fully overhauled at the factory late in 1953, then sold to a group of racing drivers in Guatemala, who entered them in the cross-Mexico Carrera Panamericana event – and promptly triumphed in the 1500 cc class! Sadly, all track was lost of these first two cars a mere two years later, and they have remained untraceable to this day.

The 550 had its first major public appearance at the Paris Motor Show. Small in size its manufacturer may have been at the time, but visitors were agreeably surprised by the stylish two-seater with Dr. Fuhrmann's complex but powerful engine, soon to propel the company's products to innumerable victories on all the world's racing circuits. Porsche was still not certain whether customers would be prepared to spend their money on an exotic product of this kind. But soon the inquiries began to roll in, and the project was approved. Another year was to elapse before the first 550-1500RS cars reached their impatient private customers. Porsche needed this time to transform hand-built prototypes into a reliable competition car for wealthy amateur racing drivers. The 550 sold for no less than 24,600 German Marks, a very considerable sum at the time.

One of the first private customers was a film star with a fast-growing reputation: James Dean. In September 1955, Porsche's importer for the West Coast of America, John von Neumann, received his first allocation of five Porsche 550 Spyders. One was destined for James Dean, at the time 24 years old and enjoying his new-found fame as a cinema super-star after three impressive films: "East of Eden", "Rebel Without a Cause" and "Giants". Dean had already taken part in several minor races with his 356 Super Speedster, not entirely without success. In his essay "Far from Eden", the American author Brook Yates describes him as follows: "Dean was short-sighted in the strict medical sense of the term, but he drove with a kind of daring enhanced by pure natural talent, crouched forwards with his head sunk. He was not just a stupid movie star interested only in impressing his friends; he may have been clumsy and over-eager, but he was certainly far from slow out there."

In fact, Dean won his very first race. His next move was an obvious one: a request to John von Neumann to trade in the Speedster for a "proper" competition car: the 550 Spyder. To quote Brook Yates again: "There was naturally some doubt as to whether Dean was experienced enough to handle this car, but on September 21 von Neumann accepted a check for 3000 dollars, and the Speedster in part-exchange, and James Dean became the proud owner of the Spyder with the production number 550-0055."

On September 30, Dean planned to drive 300 miles to Salinas for his first race in the new car, taking his mechanic Rolf Wütherich along with him. The original idea of putting the car on a truck in Malibu and heading north was soon abandoned, because Dean wanted to get to know his treasured new possession better during the journey. On Route 466, a mile from a dreary provincial settlement by the name of Cholame, the young student Donald Turnupseed failed to see

**Low weight, good aerodynamics, mid-engine, short wheelbase, rigid frame – together, they made "Number One" a notably agile car**

Most 550 Spyders were sold to private entrants in the USA, whose successes did much to establish Porsche's high reputation in that country.

The last 550A factory entry was on January 26th, 1958 in the Buenos Aires 1000-kilometer race: Stirling Moss and Jean Behra achieved a sensational third place overall.

the approaching Porsche and turned left into Route 41 across its path. Dean, Wütherich and the 550 Spyder had no chance of avoiding him.

Dean died within a few minutes, Wütherich survived until 1981 but never recovered properly from his injuries. The man who overlooked James Dean's car so completely was not prosecuted – his statement to the police was simply that he had never seen the silver Porsche as it approached.

Those were also the days when every factory prototype provided its designers with new information after each successive race, so that no car was identical either technically or visually with the one before. The version to be supplied to customers was therefore subjected to much fine detailing in Stuttgart Technical University's wind tunnel and in the company's own development department, before the Wendler company in Reutlingen finally received a specification for the bodies it had been commissioned to build. About 70 cars of this type were sold, so that the decision to build the 550 not only paid off in terms of prestige (the list of racing successes grew longer every week) but also as a return on the initial financial investment.

As is so often the case, however, "the better is the enemy of the good" – and the engineers had plenty of ideas on how to make the 550 even faster. In the spring of 1956, the Porsche works team thus appeared on the racing circuits with a much-improved Spyder, the 550A, which rapidly set the standard in the 1.5-liter class. This model was initially unavailable to private entrants.

The most significant change was a totally new tubular space frame chassis, representing an almost ideal combination of high strength and low weight. There was also a new steering box and a completely redesigned rear suspension. Racing driver Ken Miles commented as follows: "The end result of the modifications was an almost incredible improvement in handling. The car's provocative oversteer was a thing of the past; the RS was suddenly as docile to drive as one could possibly have wished." To match these changes, power output was boosted to as much as 135 bhp at 7200 rpm, so that the engine had no problems at all in propelling the 550A (which now weighed only 530 kilograms) in a most impressive manner.

Once again, Porsche began to carry off a series of class wins – on the Nürburgring, in Le Mans, in Buenos Aires. It is therefore no wonder that private entrants clamored to be allowed to purchase the 550A. Porsche gave way in due course and together with the Wendler company produced a further 14 cars by the end of 1956. In the following year, customers with sufficient wealth at their disposal took delivery of a further 23 Spyders.

On January 26, 1958 Stirling Moss and Jean Behra secured a sensational third place overall in the Buenos Aires 1000 km race. This was to be the final works entry for this, Porsche's first out-and-out-competition car. From then on, the many private owners took over and assured a continuing flow of outright wins and other excellent placings all over the world.

**The 550A's first racing appearances were in the spring of 1956 – here for instance at the start of the notorious "Mille Miglia".**

Porsche Number One and the 550 have remained the classics in Porsche's design repertoire until this very day, thanks to their elegant simplicity and the sheer efficiency with which they interpret the traditional maxim that "Form follows Function". Not surprisingly, many people felt themselves reminded very strongly of these distinguished ancestors when the Boxster design study was first unveiled. Technical experts and designers alike have done much to make these links with the past manifest, in both visual and engineering terms. And this is without doubt the right approach: any concept that helped to establish a company with a worldwide reputation surely deserves to be re-interpreted in modern form.

JÜRGEN LEWANDOWSKI

Air inlets as a common styling feature, but with different functions: on the Boxster, they feed air to the oil coolers, whereas forty years before they were an urgent necessity to keep the brakes cool.

Such a meeting shows all four of them in the best possible light: the Spyder from the 1950s, the Boxster for the next millennium - but also Hans and Walter. The comparison itself emphasizes the individual details of the cars.

# Meeting Points

The sweeping curves of time, geography, Porsche and two lives with Porsche. Recently, they all came together again: Hans Herrmann, Walter Röhrl, the Spyder and the Boxster.

A life with Porsche is by no means a mere mechanical existence. People can lead a Porsche life alongside a number of other lives, and with luck, these various layers will fit together beautifully to form a tasty dream sandwich of exciting experiences. Forgive this somewhat wild metaphor from an otherwise talented author who savors the juicy, mouth-watering thought of nibbling his way appreciatively through to 1970.

That was the year in which the Porsche life curves of Hans Herrmann and Walter Röhrl came closest together.

Herrmann was 42, with a career of rallies, road and Grand Prix races spanning eighteen years behind him. In the process, he had provided motor sport photography with one of its most exciting moments by parting company with his up-ended Formula 1 BRM at 290 km/h, performing sixteen somersaults in all. That was on the Avus in 1959, and one thing is certain: it taught him to appreciate the joys of life in ways a trainee baker could never have imagined.

Walter Röhrl was 23 at the time, and working for the Bishop of Regensburg. He already knew a little about these joys of life, having let a friend talk him into a few rallies, where he attracted attention in the strangest way: he didn't fit into any of the common categories.

Meanwhile, this friend of Walter Röhrl had invested 15,000 marks in a 911 which was ex-Safari Rally, ex-Barth and ex-just about everything, with 110,000 kilometers on the clock. The two of them took it on the Bavarian Rally, which counted towards the Mitropa Cup and therefore even attracted a certain Sandro Munari. Röhrl, the unknown rally revolution, won all five of the special tests until a half-shaft gave up, and his lead never fell below 25 seconds. A report on this appeared in "rallye racing", a works Capri was offered and the inevitable took its course.

At that time Hans Herrmann was taking part in the Le Mans 24-hour race, which was savaged by brutal rain in 1970: "... it fell like thick curtains from the sky. The rain battered at the windshield like hail, as if somebody had hurled a bucket of water against it." This made conditions, shall we say, rather delicate for a Porsche 917, and the victory was a masterpiece of bravery and skill in defeating the elements. Hans Herrmann announced his retirement the day after his triumph, and reflects on it today as "an excellent decision."

The sweeping curves of time, geography, Porsche and two lives with Porsche: now let them all come together for a meeting in the present.

26 years have gone by, and Walter Röhrl and Hans Herrmann have become older, calmer and wiser. The Le Mans 917 has found a home in the Porsche museum, while the Bavaria Rally 911 is lost in the sands of time.

We're in Tuscany, with the scent of hibiscus, Pecorino and the Mille Miglia in the air, and the very latest Porsche is on the road.

The Boxster has traveled back in time to meet its alter ego, the phenomenal, legendary Spyder from midway through the nineteen-fifties.

The legend is of course outshone by the immortal James Dean, who will never drive anything other than the little Spyder. The history of the car itself has been forgotten along the way, but its role was a great one:

Porsche first entered the fast lane of motor sport with the Spyder 550.

Porsche finally left behind its VW evolution phase with the Spyder 550:

The legendary "Fuhrmann engine" with four camshafts driven by two vertical shafts was the first power unit designed by Porsche for Porsche.

Like Röhrl, Hans Herrmann did not believe in hanging around: he indulged in a little rally driving which caused the world to catch its breath, followed by speedy success in the works team.

Since both were just beginning to blossom, Hans Herrmann quickly found himself growing attached to the Porsche 550. Everything ran like a dream right from the start, even his relationship with this exceptionally light car. As it happened, the official project number matched the car's weight, and at just 550 kilograms, it behaved in some remarkable ways:

"The front of the car had a tendency to lift very easily when racing," recalls Hans Herrmann. "There were sections

**The essence of the Spyder is still full of vibrant life in the Boxster, though with its own independent character**

like Maison Blanche at Le Mans or the Pflanzgarten at the Ring, where you couldn't feel a thing at the front, as if you were going to take off any second. You could really set yourself apart from other drivers when the car lifted on those long bends: you had to drive in a very precise way if you wanted to keep your foot down. Genuinely taking off was not really likely, though; that was reserved for aerodynamics in later years."

And so Hans Herrmann grew up with the 550, and they matured together. When Hans ended up in hospital after an accident (with another make, incidentally), Porsche brought in a famous Grand Prix driver to drive the 550 in the Eifel race. He had severe problems with setting up the car, so guess what Doctor Fuhrmann did?

"Give Hans a call in hospital, tell him to get over here if he can."

At the hospital, they made him sign a piece of paper and bandaged him up particularly well. Hans scratched out the right gear ratios on a table in the workshop, and the next day he was the fastest in practice. That's the way things went in the nineteen-fifties.

Of course, the wind played with the small, light car, and Hans recalls that there was no point in getting upset about it. It was up to you if you wanted to be friends with the wind or not, "and if you took the car up to 7000 rpm on the Hunaudières straight, getting ready to hit Mulsanne at 230 km/h, then you had to think and steer with every gust of wind. You had to be very careful, since anything could happen when you were slowing down, and you had to give in to a heavy gust and steer into it. Otherwise, you'd be in the forest before the gust ended."

Spyder meets Boxster. "Both of them look great, each in its own way," says Röhrl. "The comparison itself emphasizes each of their best points. Just look at these two silver paint jobs. The difference in color is quite small, but the enthusiast could easily get carried away."

**A notable performance by the Spyder 550: Hans Herrmann wins his class in the 1954 Mille Miglia.**

It is hard to capture the difference between the two silver paint finishes, Zermatt (old) and Polar (new), despite the most expensive printing technology. But you can sense it, depending on how the light catches the cars, and the Tuscany sun catches them superbly.

There's no need to emphasize what the two have in common after four decades. Says Röhrl, "It's wonderful to see how the essence of the Spyder has been taken further in the Boxster, with its own identity and character. Both of them convey two main messages: mid-engine, Porsche family. It's like the same chocolates in a different box."

Hans Herrmann sees a similarity that takes him back in time: the front air ducts are now there for styling reasons and to feed air to the two oil coolers, but "in those days, they were absolutely vital for the brakes. We just couldn't get enough air to them."

Perhaps the most important symbol in the history of the Porsche company - and we're not talking about the mythical imponderabilities of James Dean on 30th September 1955 – was the result of a single race involving the 550 Spyder. The drivers? Hans Herrmann and Jaroslav Juhan.

It was during the Carrera Panamericana of 1954 that the little Spyder with its 1500 cc engine broke the stranglehold of the powerful Ferraris and came in 3rd and 4th overall. Hans Herrmann beat the class record by an incredible four-and-a-half hours.

This result was so sensational that Porsche decided to retain the name "Carrera" in future years, thereby opening a second product line. The first car to bear the name "Carrera" was a 100 bhp version of the 356 (normal power output: 44 to 75 bhp) in 1955.

The new name became a neat and convincing way of distinguishing between Porsches fitted with regular engines and those featuring four-camshaft units.

But we're not in Mexico now, we're on the Mille Miglia route. It goes without saying that this too was a glorious run for the 550. Herrmann and Linge won in their class in 1954, coming sixth overall behind Lancia, Ferrari and Maserati cars driven by all-time greats such as Ascari, Marzotto and Musso.

It's fabulous to hear Hans Herrmann talking about the good old days:

"With 117 horsepower and a lightweight car, we did well in the mountains and through the bends, but naturally we had no chance when it came to the long straights in the Rimini and Pescara regions. Herbert Linge and I had what I would refer to as our bible – a ring binder full of symbols which we had prepared during training. Obviously, we made use of this sign language, and the most striking thing we had was the red card. When Linge showed it me, I knew exactly what it meant: FOR HEAVEN'S SAKE, SLOW DOWN, SLOW DOWN!

We oriented ourselves according to particular features of the route, the most important of which were level crossings. Anything was possible on those. Sometimes they were indeed level and could be taken at full speed, sometimes they rose well above the road and we had to cross them at 40 kilometers an hour.

The Mille Miglia rule for the barriers was that they should be shut at the very last moment, when the train was close, and this would be indicated by someone waving a flag.

On one occasion we came to a 160 km/h right-hand bend with a level crossing immediately behind it – with the barriers down! But the man with the flag was standing behind the bend rather than in front of it, and by the time we saw the closed barriers, we had no chance of stopping. From the corner of my eye I saw that the train was not quite there and I shoved Linge's head down. Dive! The train went through about half a second after we drove under the barriers, and Linge didn't comment much on anything else for quite a while after that."

Three years later came the dreadful accident involving spectators, and it was curtains for the Mille Miglia. Walter Röhrl was just ten at the time.

Consequently, Röhrl's only chance to join in the fun was the Historic Mille Miglia, and in 1993 he was entered in a Spyder 550 A dating from 1956. The Porsche museum had installed a particularly meaty version of the Fuhrmann engine, delivering 143 bhp. "The result was a sensational racing engine," says Röhrl's co-pilot Helmut Zwickl. "At between 7000 and 8000 revs, it could blow even Walter's socks off. But when we were traveling in third gear at 4000 rpm, the four-cylinder Boxer sent every single ignition pulse right to our brain. Our aluminum speedboat was spluttering for at least 30 of the 32 hours we spent in it. Walter nursed it along with his big toe and nudged it up a thousand times to 4000 rpm in third gear, by which time we were doing about 100 km/h. It would cough and belch its way up to 5000 revs, and that's when the real cacophony began. Only at 6500 revs did the earsplitting noise subside, and we always felt we could hear the spark plugs rejoicing as if they and the pistons had just been ceremonially cleansed for the first time."

Somewhere in the mountains, Walter put his foot down, and progress was excellent through the Futa pass. The Spyder caught up with a modern RS belonging to a fan; the RS stepped up the pressure, whereupon Röhrl did so too, overtaking on the outside of a 170 km/h bend and departing at high speed. The RS reached the end of the test section a minute and a half later, and the driver lowered his window in annoyance which changed immediately to relief:

"Thank God. IT'S RÖHRL!"

"As a modern driver, you very quickly feel a certain lack of precision," says Röhrl about his experience behind the wheel of the 550. "But once you've overcome that, the car becomes quite stable and has sufficient cornering power. There is actually very little mass to push you outwards. The old Dunlop Racing 15-inch tires feel at home on this lightweight car."

His most lasting impression is of the exhaust pipe on the special Spyder, which had never seen any kind of muffler." The noise was so infernal that you could not imagine the car being used anywhere except on the Mille Miglia. The intensity and frequency were even enough to activate the anti-theft alarms on cars parked at the roadside. Nee-naa nee-naa, here comes Röhrl!"

There are plenty more stories about life with the Porsche Spyder, and the new Boxster is a glorious opportunity to recall some of them. Hans Herrmann will now tell us one for the road, about the team's homecoming from the Targa Florio race in 1956:

"We only entered when Huschke von Hanstein discovered that the Targa offered the second-best prize money in the world after Indianapolis. So we loaded a 550 onto a trailer and sent it off with two mechanics, Werner and Willi. Umberto Maglioli and Huschke were meant to take turns driving, but somehow it didn't work out that way, and Maglioli drove the race right through to the end, with victory over the three-liter Maserati and Ferrari 860 Monza. It was fantastic. The first overall victory for Porsche! Of course, enthusiasm in Germany was just as great, and when the winners returned to Stuttgart, people came out into the streets to greet them. Work stopped at the Zuffenhausen plant for the first time and the workers poured out to celebrate their victorious team. And do you know how impressive a winning team looked in those days? Huschke and Umberto were on the trailer with their little Porsche Spyder, being towed by Werner and Willi in an Opel Blitz: that was it, the complete power behind a historic victory."

**Two messages: mid-engine, Porsche family. Like a mountain panorama, different from various viewpoints but with the same commanding peaks**

HERBERT VÖLKER

That's all on the subject of ellipses: our very own cavaliers, the designers, assure us that variations in geometry give rise to motion in still-practical forms too. Film actress Sonja Kirchberger evidently agrees.

Hélène is from France, Carlo from America, Sonja from Austria. The most delightful little cookery school you could imagine brought them together: "La Bottega del 30" in the Villa a Sesta, almost within the long shadow cast by the castle at San Gusmè, east of Siena.

It was a glorious day in Pienza, where the old town's small cobbled streets are open to some unusual guests, and even in the square in front of the cathedral the young men were contemplating the beauty of the modern age. And on the way home, the silhouettes. San Felice!

There are no such things as cars for women or cars for men, and bearing this in mind one should finally stop discriminating against men, who sometimes, in fact more and more often, have shown themselves capable of good taste.

# The Practical Application of Beauty

Photographing Sonja Kirchberger is a reasonable contribution to the subject of aesthetics. With a Boxster in the picture, it's even better, and the Tuscan light adds to the harmony.

"**D**o you guys want a road movie?" the actress asked. "No," said the wise photographer, whose assistant's name is Manitou – which can't just be a coincidence. "No," he said, "for road movies you have to make something up, and we won't be making anything up this week." And so it all turned out just as simple as Tuscan bread. Completely unsalted, it serves the higher honor of the essential. The spices and aromas of Tuscany make it complete – the aroma of the food, the oil, the drinks. "Tuscany is the light of Europe," the photographer said – this was the screenplay, by and large, with Sonja Kirchberger exhibiting her usual beauty, and the Boxster exhibiting its usual beauty too.

A statement without rehearsal? "I like the proportions of the Boxster, they are surprising. The hard top is perhaps the most surprising feature, because it gives the car an identity of its own," says Sonja Kirchberger. "The details of the car have a delicate finesse that is good for the imagination and makes the car enjoyable, but there is also something about it that gives you the same safe feeling as traveling by rail, the feeling that nothing will knock it off its track. And the rear end is just great, you don't have to explain that any further, do you?" The question about what we used to call the women's angle leads to a modern, short answer. "There are no men's cars and women's cars, that's just an old boring story from the early days of the automobile. The time has really come to stop discriminating against men, since sometimes – more and more often – they do have good taste. So they also buy attractive cars. Women do that anyway, if they have a choice."

A ghosted view of the Boxster shows the immense attention to detail that Porsche's engineers in Weissach have devoted to its technical layout. Every design feature bears the stamp of pure Porsche technology.

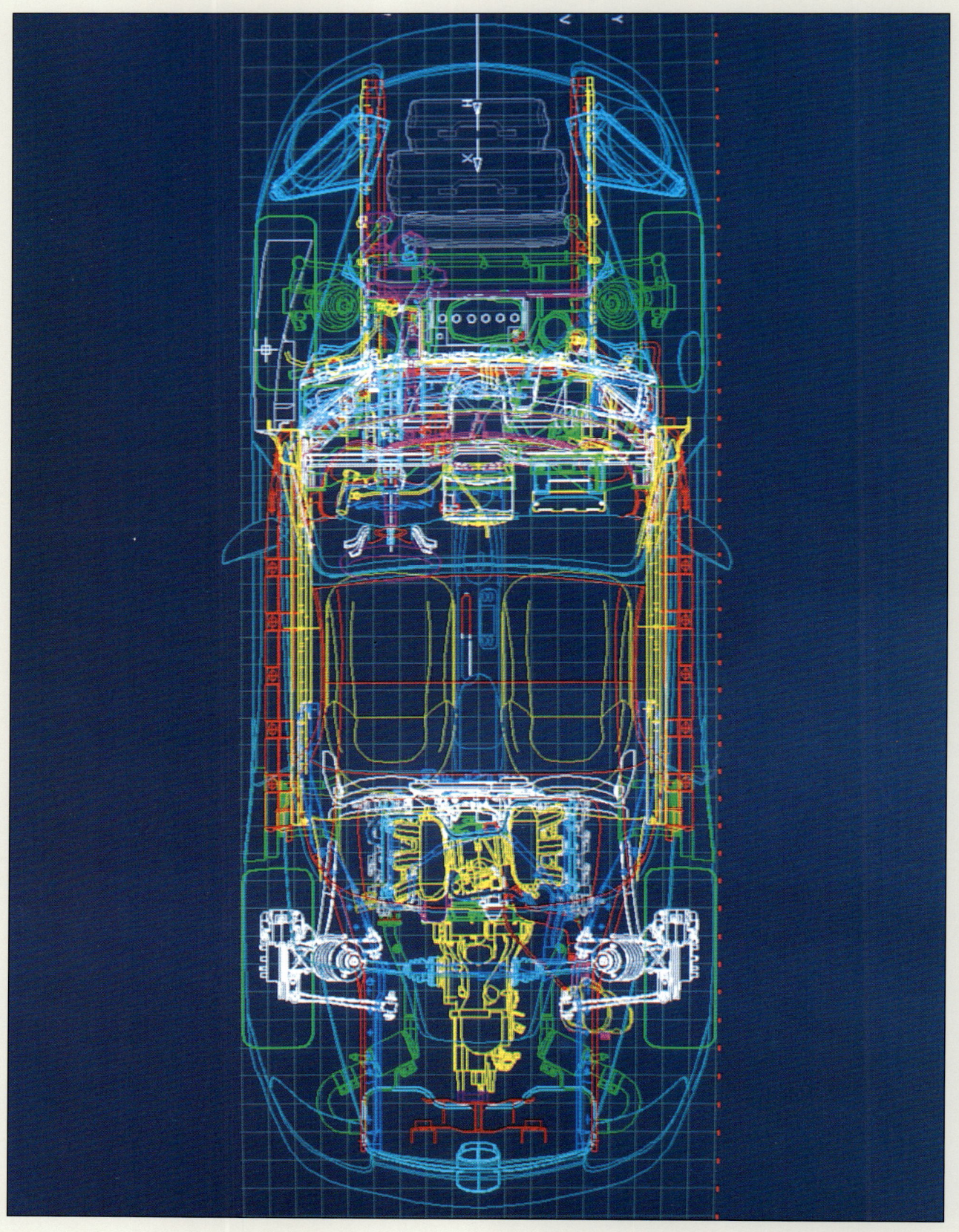

# Technical Data

## Engine
| | | |
|---|---|---|
| Number of cylinders | | 6 |
| Bore | mm (in) | 85.5 (3.4) |
| Stroke | mm (in) | 72 (2.8) |
| Displacement | cc (cu. in) | 2480 (151.3) |
| Compression ratio | | 11.0 : 1 |
| Max. output | kW (bhp/SAE hp) | 150 (204/201) |
| - at engine speed | rpm | 6000 |
| Max. torque | Nm (kpm) | 245 (25) |
| - at engine speed | rpm | 4500 |

## Engine design
Type: 6 cylinders, horizontally opposed, aluminum block, water-cooled

Valves: 2 overhead inlet valves, parallel, in V pattern
2 overhead exhaust valves, parallel, in V pattern

Exhaust emission control: Oxygen sensing (lambda probe) and closed-loop, three-way catalytic converter (metal monolith)
USA: additional electric secondary air injection pump

## Fuel consumption   liters/100 km
| | Manual shift | Tiptronic |
|---|---|---|
| - acc. to DIN 93/116 test | | |
| Town | 14.3 | 15.8 |
| Country | 7.1 | 8.1 |
| Total | 9.7 | 10.9 |
| - acc. to DIN 89/491 test | | |
| Urban cycle | 12.2 | 13.0 |
| Steady 90 kph | 6.3 | 6.7 |
| Steady 120 kph | 8.1 | 8.4 |
| Average of above 3 tests | 8.9 | 9.4 |

## Electrical system
| | |
|---|---|
| Battery capacity   Amp/h/Amps | |
| - manual shift, without air conditioning | 60/280 |
| - Tiptronic, manual shift with air conditioning | 70/340 |
| Ignition | D M E, individual coils, knock control, |
| Firing order | 1 - 6 - 2 - 4 - 3 - 5 |

## Driveline
Engine and gearbox bolted together to form a single unit. Drive to rear wheels by double universal-joint shafts

Clutch (manual-shift cars): Single dry plate, hydraulic operation, double-mass flywheel

Transmission:
| | Manual shift | Tiptronic |
|---|---|---|
| Number of gears (fwd./rev.) | 5/1 | 5/1 |
| Ratios (i) 1st | 3.50 | 3.66 |
| 2nd | 2.12 | 2.00 |
| 3rd | 1.43 | 1.41 |
| 4th | 1.03 | 1.00 |
| 5th | 0.79 | 0.74 |
| Reverse | 3.44 | 4.10 |
| Final drive ratio (i) | 3.89 | 4.205* |

\* Intermediate reduction ratio: 1.25
Axle: 3.36

## Chassis and suspension
Front: Independent, wishbones, longitudinal links and McPherson struts (Porsche-optimized)

Rear: Independent, wishbones, longitudinal links, track rods and McPherson struts (Porsche-optimized)

## Steering
| | | |
|---|---|---|
| Steering wheel diameter | mm (in) | 380 (14.96) |
| Turning circle (overall) | m (ft) | 10.0 (35.8) |
| Turning circle (wheels) | m (ft) | 10.28 (33.7) |

## Brakes
Service brake: Pedal operated, hydraulic with mechanical linkage, dual circuit (front/rear split), ventilated front and rear disks, ABS standard, Traction Control (TC) optional, provision for change-over to automatic braking differential (ABD)

## Wheels and tires
Summer tires:
| | |
|---|---|
| Size, front (tire – wheel) | 205/55 ZR 16 – 6 J x 16 |
| Size, rear (tire – wheel) | 225/50 ZR 16 – 7 J x 16 |

Alternatively:
| | |
|---|---|
| Size, front (tire – wheel) | 205/50 ZR 17 – 7 J x 17 |
| Size, rear (tire – wheel) | 225/40 ZR 17 – 8.5 J x 17 |

Winter tires:
| | |
|---|---|
| Size, front (tire – wheel) | 205/55 R16 89T M+S – 6 J x 16 |
| Size, rear (tire – wheel) | 225/50 R16 92T M+S – 7 J x 16 |

Temporary spare wheel:
| | |
|---|---|
| High-pressure tire | T105/95 R17 |
| Wheel | 3.5 J x 17 |

## Dimensions
| | | |
|---|---|---|
| Length | mm (in) | 4315 (170.0) |
| Length USA | mm (in) | 4340 (171.0) |
| Width | mm (in) | 1780 (70.1) |
| Height | mm (in) | 1290 (50.8) at DIN unladen wt. |
| Wheelbase | mm (in) | 2415 (95.2) |

## Weights
Unladen weight, depending on equipment

Manual shift
| | | | |
|---|---|---|---|
| Front | kg (lbs) | 585... 620 | (1290...1367) |
| Rear | kg (lbs) | 665... 700 | (1466...1543) |
| Total | kg (lbs) | 1250...1320* | (2756...2910) |

Tiptronic
| | | | |
|---|---|---|---|
| Front | kg (lbs) | 585... 620 | (1290...1367) |
| Rear | kg (lbs) | 715... 750 | (1576...1653) |
| Total | kg (lbs) | 1300...1370* | (2866...3020) |

*EU-registration: plus 75 kg (165 lbs) for driver, 35 kg (77 lbs) on front axle, 40 kg (88 lbs) on rear axle,

Axle load limits
| | | Manual shift | Tiptronic |
|---|---|---|---|
| Front | kg (lbs) | 775 (1799) | 775 (1799) |
| Rear | kg (lbs) | 895 (1973) | 895 (1973) |
| Gross weight limit | kg (lbs) | 1560 (3439) | 1610 (3549) |

## Fuel tank
| | | |
|---|---|---|
| Capacity | liters (Imp./US gal.) | 58 (12.8/15.3) |
| - including reserve of liters (Imp./US gal.) | | 9 (2.0/2.4) |

## Performance
| | | Manual shift | | Tiptronic | |
|---|---|---|---|---|---|
| Top speed | kph (mph) | 240 (149) | | 235 (146) | |
| Acceleration | | | | | |
| 0–100 kph | s | 6.9 | sec. | 7.6 | s |
| 0–60 mph | s | 6.7 | sec. | 7.4 | s |
| 0–160 kph (app. 100 mph) | s | 16.5 | sec. | 18.9 | s |
| Standing-start kilometer | s | 27.4 | sec. | 28.0 | s |
| Standing-start quarter-mile | s | 15.1 | sec. | 15.5 | s |

## Pictures

Christoph Bauer: Pages 10/11, 14/15, 22/23, 24/25, 26/27, 28/29, 32/33, 34, 39, 55, 60/61, 62/63, 64/65, 68/69, 76/77, 78, 79 (2), 80/81, 82, 83, 84/85, 88, 89 (2), 95, 100.

Dieter Blum: Pages 18/19, 30/31, 40/41, 42/43, 44/45, 46, 48/49, 50, 51 (2), 52/53, 54 (2), 56, 58, 59, 66, 67 (2), 70 (2), 71 (2), 72, 73, 74 (3), 75, 86/87, 90/91, 92, 93 (2), 94, 97, 132/133, 134/135, 136/137, 138/139, 140/141, 142/143, 144, 145 (2), 146/147, 148/149, 150/151, 152, 153, 154, 155, 158.

Peter Vann: Pages 12/13, 20/21, 118/119, 120/121, 122/123, 124/125, 126/127, 128.

Michel de Vries: Page 130

Porsche works photos: Pages 16/17, 36 (3), 37 (3), 38 (3), 47 (2), 57, 98 (3), 99 (3), 102/103, 104/105, 106/107, 108/109, 110/111, 112, 113, 114, 115, 116, 117, 156/157.